Casemate Short History

D1169291

GREEK WARRIORS

HOPLITES AND HEROES

Carolyn Willekes

CASEMATE
Oxford & Philadelphia

Published in Great Britain and
the United States of America in 2017 by
CASEMATE PUBLISHERS
The Old Music Hall, 106–108 Cowley Road, Oxford OX4 1JE, UK
1950 Lawrence Road, Havertown, PA 19083, USA

© Casemate Publishers 2017

Paperback Edition: ISBN 978-1-61200-515-7
Digital Edition: ISBN 978-1-61200-516-4 (epub)

Printed in the Czech Republic by FINIDR, s.r.o.
Typeset in India by Lapiz Digital Services, Chennai

For a complete list of Casemate titles, please contact:

CASEMATE PUBLISHERS (UK)
Telephone (01865) 241249
Email: casemate-uk@casematepublishers.co.uk
www.casematepublishers.co.uk

CASEMATE PUBLISHERS (US)
Telephone (610) 853-9131
Fax (610) 853-9146
Email: casemate@casematepublishers.com
www.casematepublishers.com

CONTENTS

INTRODUCTION

It is impossible to talk about the Greek warrior without first understanding the land he came from. The role and development of warfare in the Greek world was very much dictated by the environment. The climate is one of hot, dry summers and mild, wet winters, but the weather can be unexpectedly violent, with wind and rain systems wreaking havoc on the land. Greece is defined by mountains and islands and has no navigable rivers. The numerous mountain chains criss-cross the mainland and split it into different regions, like Attica, Argos, Boeotia, Lacedaemonia, Thessaly, Macedonia, Arcadia, etc. In addition to mainland Greece there are hundreds of islands, with Crete and Euboea being the largest. Travel between the islands was possible during the summer months, but for the rest of the year the Mediterranean becomes an unpredictable and tempestuous sea. This combination of mountains and islands created a degree of isolation, which in turn led to the development of unique and individual territories. In other words, although the inhabitants of the Greek world all spoke the same language (though with different dialects), used the same alphabet, and worshipped the same gods, they were never actually a unified country under a single centralized government. Instead, each region created its own legal codes, political system, and military, and this is central to our understanding of Greek warfare and how it worked. Rather than uniting under a common entity acting on behalf of greater Greece, each state acted in their own self-interest. The inhabitants of the ancient Greek world rarely saw themselves as 'Hellenes', only in times of crisis, like during the Persian Wars, did any sense of national identity appear; and even then not every state joined in. Instead, individuals viewed themselves as citizens of the state they lived in: they were Athenian, Spartan, Argive, Theban, not 'Greek'. This absence of unity was the biggest influence on Greek warfare, as each state had no qualms about fighting its neighbour for personal gain. It also led to a never-ending series of shifting alliances, a particularly influential factor during the Peloponnesian War. The concept of Panhellenism (all Greek) did exist in the ancient world. The Olympics were one of the Panhellenic games, only open to Greek citizens; and the term was a favourite of orators, politicians, and generals: both Philip II and Alexander the Great pitched their invasion of Persia as a Panhellenic crusade. It was a handy term, but far from an actual reality.

Compounding the isolation created by topography was the lack of arable land. Greece is not a particularly fertile region, and open plains are difficult to find. This lack of farmland placed a lot of pressure on the state, particularly when populations began to grow during the Archaic period. This led to a period of intense colonization as states sent out groups of citizens to establish colonies. Although the colonies spread across Southern Europe, North Africa, and the coastal Near East, the two most extensively colonized regions were Southern Italy and Sicily – a region known as Magna Graecia (Greater Greece) – and the Black Sea. These colonies developed their own governments and acted as independent entities, but they maintained ties to their mother city, which they could call upon in times of stress or danger. Sparta, as we shall see, did things differently. Rather than colonising – they only founded one major colony: Tarentum in southern Italy – they conquered, invading their neighbours to directly add to their own territory. The ramifications of this are discussed later in this chapter.

Warfare in the ancient world was not static, but perpetually changing and evolving. These changes were direct reflections of shifts in socio-political conditions. The kingdoms of the Bronze Age world fielded aristocratic warriors with their war chariots and an emphasis on single combat. The warriors of the Bronze Age are intertwined with the heroes of myth, men like Achilles, Odysseus, Ajax, Theseus, and Hercules. Our knowledge of Bronze Age fighting techniques is hazy, as our main source is Homer, who recounts part of the siege at Troy in his *Iliad*. This is problematic as Homer wrote the *Iliad* several hundred years after the fall of Troy; moreover, he was writing down a story that had been part of an oral tradition for centuries. Thus, we often stumble across passages that seem to describe the style of fighting used in Homer's own day, rather than that of the Bronze Age Mycenaean world. The collapse of these kingdoms led to a period in Greek History known as the Dark Ages, during which the inhabitants of the Greek world became more inward looking. This all changed with the start of Archaic Greece, Homer's own period, which was defined by the rise of the city state and extensive colonization. The Greek warrior as we know him is a product of this period. He was not a soldier of Greece, but of his state. Some regions were renowned for producing a certain type of warrior or excelling at a particular style of fighting: Sparta for hoplites, Thessaly for cavalry, Athens for its navy. The men who made up these armed forces were citizens of their state, and as such, that is where their loyalties lay. This book focuses on these citizen armies and their role in shaping the course of Greek history. We will look at three formative periods: the Persian Wars, the Peloponnesian War, the rise of Macedon under Philip II and his son, Alexander the Great, and his subsequent conquest of Asia.

Infantry

When we think of Greek warfare there is one warrior that comes to mind above all others: the hoplite. These 'men of bronze' were the heavy infantry of antiquity, who marched to battle in their disciplined and densely packed formations known as a phalanx. Equipped with a large round shield, spear and sword, wearing a crested helmet and body armour, the hoplite was the iconic Greek warrior. They were the heart of the Archaic and Classical armies. These men were citizen soldiers who fought for their state. The hoplite as we know him first appears in the Archaic period, at a time of great change in the Greek world with the birth of the city-state (the *polis*) and a new citizen identity within them. New forms of government and civic structure naturally led to a re-thinking of the army and how to fight a war. No longer did top honours go to the aristocratic warrior, riding to battle in his chariot and fighting in single combat against his equals for his personal honour and prestige. Now it was the citizen group fighting together as a cohesive unit who won glory, not for the individual, but for the state.

The armament of the hoplite was as iconic as the man himself. His primary weapon was the *dory*, a spear measuring 2–2.5m in length, tipped at each end with a bronze or iron spearhead and butt spike. This weapon could be used both for the offensive and defensive, thrusting over the shields on the attack, or firmly planted in the ground against a charge.

As a secondary weapon he carried the *xiphos*, a single-handed sword with a double-edged, leaf-shaped blade that measured on average 50–60cm in length. The shape of the *xiphos'* blade made is suitable for both thrusting and cutting, while its short length was ideal for use within the confines of the phalanx. The namesake of the hoplite, however, was his shield, the *hoplon*. This was a large, round, convex shield measuring approximately 90cm in diameter and weighing 7kg. It was made of wood and faced with bronze. The hoplite carried his *hoplon* on his left arm, holding it by means of an armband and handle. On account

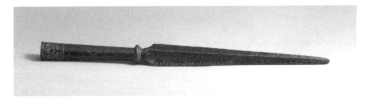

Bronze butt spike from a hoplite spear. (Metropolitan Museum of Art Open Content Program)

Bronze Corinthian helmet. The full face design offered protection, but restricted visibility. (Metropolitan Museum of Art Open Content Program)

of its size, the *hoplon* was able to cover the hoplite from shoulder to knee. The shield offered a great deal of protection but on account of how it was carried, the right side of the hoplite was somewhat exposed. To counter this, the hoplite could tuck in behind the left side of the shield held by the man next to him. While the shield was primarily a defensive tool, and formed the basis for the layout of the hoplite phalanx, it could also be used as an attacking weapon. For protective armour, the hoplite wore a helmet: they are usually depicted wearing the full face Corinthian style with a horsehair plume waving above.

The Corinthian style helmet offered a considerable degree of protection and it gave the hoplite an inhuman appearance, as only they eyes and mouth were visible, but it did restrict the bearer's awareness of his surroundings. The conical shaped,

Armourer making a Corinthian helmet. Hoplite equipment was costly and the majority of citizens could not afford a full panoply. (Metropolitan Museum of Art Open Content Program)

open-faced helmet was also popular and gave a much better range of vision, but offered less protection.

In artistic representations the hoplite almost always wears a breastplate/corselet. These could be made of bronze or leather, but we also hear of a version made from layers of linen, glued together to form an early version of Kevlar. They could also wear bronze greaves to protect their shins and calves, as these were exposed below the shield. This then, is the typical image we have of the hoplite panoply. Reality, however, was quite different.

A hoplite had to purchase his own arms and armour, and this was expensive. Hoplites were not professional soldiers; they fought for the *polis* but were not in the full-time employ of the state. Thus, there was a remarkable lack of homogeneity in the

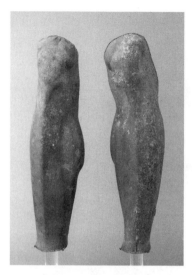

Pair of bronze greaves in a simple anatomic style. (Metropolitan Museum of Art Open Content Program)

appearance of the phalanx: every hoplite would have had his spear and his shield, but beyond that the amount and style of armour worn was dependent upon the individual and his disposable income.

It has been estimated that the full traditional hoplite panoply cost between 75–100 drachmas, which was the equivalent of 3 months pay for a skilled worker. The essential spear and shield of the hoplite cost about 25–30 drachmas: a month's wages. Mind you, these prices were for the bare bones version of the panoply, the 'workmanlike' version, if you like. If an individual had drachma to spare, well, the sky was the limit.

The armour could become as elaborate and ostentatious as the wearer desired. In other words, armour served two functions: it protected the soldier, but was also a very visible reflection of social status. Even the device painted on the front of the shield

6 obols = 1 drachma
100 drachmas = 1 mina
60 minae/6,000 drachmas = 1 talent
Average daily wage for a skilled worker = 1–1.5 drachmas

Black Figure Amphora. Hoplite donning his equipment. (Metropolitan Museum of Art Open Content Program)

was indicative of the individual. Some devices were *apotropaic*, meant to ward off evil and safeguard the bearer; others, like animal images, were meant to imbue the soldier with the physical or mental qualities of the animal, while some were just plain eccentric. Despite the apparent differences in the quality, style and amount of arms and armour used by each individual, the hoplite phalanx was nonetheless a place where social status and wealth took a back seat. A working class farmer fought alongside the wealthy man of leisure, and it was imperative that they be able to work in concert with each other. If they did not, the effectiveness and integrity of the phalanx would be compromised. The exception to the rule was Sparta with its regulation battle dress and matching shields bearing the *lambda* to represent Lacedaemonia, their home territory.

In the Spartan phalanx all hoplites, from the lowest rank to the generals, were identical in their armament, creating an even greater level of equality on the battlefield: no one Spartan ever stood out from the others. More than in any other *polis* the emphasis was on the unity of the phalanx for the greater good of the state.

The exact spacing and fighting techniques of the phalanx has been a question of some debate. On the one hand hoplite battle has often been described as something tantamount to a rugby scrum in which the ranks of hoplites are pressed up against each other as they try to shove and push the opposing phalanx back with each side shoving against the other. While this provides a particularly tangible image of hoplite warfare, it also presents some issues. If the lines were too close together, it would be difficult to wield a spear effectively, as the hoplite ran the risk of striking someone on his own side with the butt end of the weapon. Moreover, the push from behind could potentially interrupt the cohesion of the lines, particularly if one section was pushing harder than the other. Finally, those doing the pushing would be hindered in their ability to fight efficiently and effectively. There are accounts of battle that do seem to describe this crushing style of fighting, but it only seemed to happen in the throes of a particularly hard fought or desperate battle. Xenophon provides us with a particularly succinct description of hoplite combat when he writes 'So with shield pressed against shield they struggled, killed and were killed'

(Xenophon *Hellenica* 4.3.19). On the other hand, we have the idea of hoplite warfare as a disciplined advance in a tight but evenly spaced formation, with the soldiers engaging in close combat as the two sides met. This explanation allows for greater manoeuvrability and adaptability on the part of the phalanx. The solidness of the phalanx came from the placement of the shields, not the press of men. Sometimes the men advanced in a loose formation, with shield rims touching, but not overlapping, allowing a greater degree of manoeuvrability. On other occasions we hear of hoplites joining shields, which suggests a tightening of the formation with the shields overlapping and the men moving in closer together to create a more solid front. It thus seems that the hoplite phalanx could be deployed in a variety of ways, from a more open order to a tightly packed one depending on the circumstances, suggesting that hoplite battle was more fluid than often thought. The phalanx did have one notable weakness: its tendency to drift right. The reason for this is described by Thucydides in his account of the battle of Mantinea in 418:

> As they engage, all armies tend to the right, pushing out their right wing with the result that both sides then outflank their opponents' left wing with their own right. This is because each individual hoplite is anxious to bring his own undefended side as close as possible to the shield of his colleague on the right, and reckons that tight locking is the best protection. This fault is started by the line-leader of the right wing, who wants to keep his own undefended side clear of the enemy at all times, and then the others follow with the same motivation. (Thucydides 5.71.1)

As the line shifts to the right it creates gaps between the phalanx and other units on the battlefield, which the enemy could take advantage of.

The strength and force of the phalanx came not from speed, but from cohesion and a carefully managed rhythm and sense of timing. The Spartans were known for advancing in time to flute players who accompanied the phalanx, maintaining a steady and unruffled countenance, adding to their reputation as hoplites *par excellence*. Once both sides had engaged it was only the first two ranks of the phalanx who were able to strike their opponents with spears and swords. The other ranks were there to physically and mentally back up the fighters in front, to prevent the lines from being pushed backwards, and to take the place of a fallen comrade in order to maintain the unity of the phalanx.

> Let every man, then, feet set firm apart,
> Bite on his lip and stand against the foe,
> His thighs and shins, his shoulders and chest
> All hidden by the broad bulge of his shield.
> Let his right hand brandish the savage spear,
> The plume nod fearsomely above his head.
> By fierce deeds let him teach himself to fight,
> And not stand out of fire – he has a shield –
> But get in close, engage, and stab with spear
> Or sword, and strike his adversary down.
> Plant foot by enemy's foot, press shield on shield,
> Thrust helm and hem, and tangle plume with plume,
> Opposing breast to breast: that is how to fight,
> With the long lance or sword-grip in your hand.
> (Tyrtaeus 11)

Hoplite combat must have been exhausting. The battles could last anywhere from a short decisive encounter to day long affairs. Unlike the light-armed infantry and cavalry, hoplites in a phalanx could not dart in and out of battle: once the fighting commenced they had no choice but to slog through to the end. It was practically unheard of for a phalanx to enter battle, withdraw, and the return with a second wind. While false retreats were a common tactic, one used by the Spartans at Thermopylae and Philip II at Chaeronea, a real retreat signalled the end of the phalanx.

We cannot talk about hoplites without mentioning Sparta and its warrior citizens. This place and its people were largely the

Sparta and the Eurotas Valley. (C. Willekes)

result of two things: the Messenian Wars and the semi-mythical lawmaker, Lycurugus. Sparta is located in the fertile Eurotas valley with its rich alluvial plains.

Throughout the 8th century Sparta began to expand its control over Laconia, taking control of the entirety of the Eurotas valley. They then looked west over the Taygetus Mountains to the territory of Messenia. During a series of engagements known as the Messenian Wars, Sparta made a concerted effort to subjugate her neighbours. The Spartans eventually succeeded in this endeavour, but it was a hard fought struggle with defeat and setbacks for the Spartans as well as the Messenians. The subjugation of Messenia was a watershed moment in Spartan history: not only did it add considerably more arable land to their territory, they also effectively enslaved the Messenians, turning them into the helots, a serf-like population who worked, farmed etc. under the command of their Spartan overlords.

These helots were the single most important factor in the development of the Sparta that we know. This is largely for two

Spartan hoplite wearing the full traditional panoply. (R. Baylis)

reasons: the helots did all of the labour, giving the Spartans the time to focus on other things like warfare; however, the helots were also the reason Sparta became so obsessed with creating the perfect warrior. The helots vastly outnumbered the Spartan citizens, and so the Spartans lived in constant fear of a helot uprising. If such an uprising succeeded it would throw the entire Spartan way of life into complete chaos. This overriding anxiety about the helots was the foundation for many of the institutions that became enmeshed within the Spartan mystique. The creation of the Spartan legal code is attributed to Lycurugus, who may or may not have been a real person. By far the most famous of his institutions was the *agoge*: the Spartan education system, which moulded young Spartan boys into the ideal Spartan warrior. The Lycurgan laws dictated the entirety of Spartan life: living arrangements, diet, education, physical exercise, marriage, childbirth, everything was laid out within these laws. Although we associate Sparta with the hoplite, they were also master spies, perfecting the art of espionage at home with the *crypteia*, a

Spartan version of the secret police. The *crypteia* was made up of teenage Spartan boys and its purpose was to watch the helots for any possible sign of insurrection. If there was any cause for suspicion, the *crypteia* could kill, without any explanation, the suspected helots. Thus, the *crypteia* served to remove any possible instigators while also controlling the majority through terror. It also taught the teenage boys how to kill without remorse. The goal of the Lycurgan system was to create an individual who was fully dedicated to serving the state, even willing to die for it. The Spartans were famously brusque and to the point, hence our term 'laconic'. They were also terribly xenophobic, inherently suspicious of outsiders and their customs.

The Spartan government was equally unique: part monarchy, part oligarchy. They were ruled by two kings in a dual monarchy; the idea being that one would balance the other out. These kings did not have autocratic rule. The kings were shadowed by the ephors who served as their overseers. They ensured that the kings acted in a suitable Spartan manner. Every month they exchanged oaths: the kings swearing to obey the laws of Sparta and to rule

In order to achieve greater equality, **Lycurgus** is supposed to have compelled the Spartans to renounce their property and, having divided the land into equal-sized shares, redistributed the shares amongst the Spartans. To minimize greed and further promote equality, Lycurgus is said to have forbade the use of gold and silver, replacing them with bulky and heavy lumps of iron instead. Being practically worthless, and difficult to transport, this reform was seen as a way of isolating Sparta from outside trade so as to prevent foreign influence and the degradation of Spartan martial integrity.

accordingly, the ephors swearing to protects the kings' position, so long as he followed the laws. When a king marched to war, the Ephors went with him. Also essential was the *gerousia*, a council of elders (Spartan men over the age of 60) who together with the ephors acted as an equivalent of the Spartan supreme court.

The hoplite is idealized as the quintessential Greek warrior, but he was not the only infantryman on the field: he was just one component of the Greek army. This hero worship of the hoplite is not just a quirk of our modern ideologies: even in antiquity authors tended to focus on the actions and achievements of hoplites, giving only cursory mention (if any) to the other units of infantry. The light armed infantryman was the most versatile of the Greek warriors, and they often made up the bulk of the troops. There are three general categories of light armed warriors: the javelin-men, archers, and slingers; as well as the peltasts who differed from the other light armed troops as they carried a lightweight shield (the *pelta*) made of wicker or leather. Fighting as light infantry allowed a man to equip himself for combat without breaking the bank. On average a javelin cost 3 drachmas, a bow and quiver of arrows was pricier, costing about 2–3 weeks wages, while slingers literally had their ammunition at their feet, only needing to make a sling with which to fire them. Certain regions became renowned for producing a particular style of light infantry – for example; the island of Rhodes was famous for its slingers.

Sparta's monarchy was unusual in that it had two kings simultaneously. The two kings were selected from two separate bloodlines, the Agiad and the Eurypontid. According to tradition these two lines were descended from Eurysthenes and Procles respectively, descendants of Heracles who conquered the land that became Sparta after the Trojan War.

Light infantry could be deployed in variety of ways, used for scouting, skirmishing, and pitched battle, as well as on board ships. It is likely that some of the oarsmen on a trireme were also equipped to fight, and there are accounts of their participating in pitched land battles. Light infantry was particularly useful for harassing enemy hoplites. Their missile attacks did not necessarily cause any serious physical harm, but they could demoralize and fluster the enemy, causing them to waver or break the line. With their task accomplished, the light infantry could easily retreat and outpace a foolhardy charge from a hoplite phalanx, all the while taking minimal damage to themselves. Despite the numbers of light infantry in the average Hellenic army, as well as their tactical importance, we rarely hear of their accomplishments. This was due in part to the social status of the light infantry, as many of these men were from the lower economic classes, but this was not the only reason, the weapons they used also had a particular reputation. Javelins, arrows, and stones were long range missiles and as such considered a coward's tool. 'Real' infantry fought in hand to hand combat, facing their opponents in close quarters on the battlefield, rather than harassing them from a safe distance. In reality, the light infantry were viewed with such disdain because of their effectiveness: they could dart in and out of battle, appearing and disappearing with ease. The hoplite phalanx never knew where or when to expect such an attack, and it must have made them feel vulnerable. As the authors of our ancient texts would all have belonged either to the hoplite or cavalry classes, it is not surprising that they are dismissive of the 'lowly' but effective light-armed infantryman.

Cavalry

Greece is, for the most part, not ideal horse country. It is a land of mountains. Aside from a few areas like Thessaly, Macedonia, and the plains of Eretria on Euboea, there is not a lot of open grassland, a prerequisite for large scale breeding and raising of

Red Figure Column Crater: Two horsemen in traveling garb. Note the relaxed pose of both riders. (Metropolitan Museum of Art Open Content Program)

horses. Nonetheless, the horse had a place in Greek warfare from the Bronze Age onwards, and its role became increasingly important through the centuries.

The most obvious role for cavalry in pitched battle was to engage with enemy cavalry. This was done primarily to support and protect the phalanx, which is why cavalry was often placed on the wings of the army. Once drawn up for battle, the phalanx becomes a relatively rigid formation, its composition does not allow for any rapid change of direction. This made the flanks and rear of the phalanx vulnerable to attack, particularly from enemy cavalry. The mobility and speed of the cavalry allowed them to use several different formations on the battlefield, but the most common for attacking infantry were the wedge and the rhomboid.

Both of these formations ended in a pointed shape, which was used to pierce through any gaps in the enemy line and to widen them as the rest of the horsemen pushed through. Hence why the phalanx flanks were so vulnerable to cavalry: natural gaps already existed between the ranks, and these could easily be exploited if the cavalry could close in on them. As the phalanx was the bulwark of the Greek army, it was imperative that it be able to advance against the enemy without having to worry about its vulnerable sides. If these defenses broke, the phalanx could find itself vulnerable and at risk of being overrun.

In classical warfare the cavalry essentially served two central functions: they were to prevent enemy cavalry from breaking their phalanx, while at the same time trying to break through the enemy cavalry to attack the opposing phalanx. Essentially, the phalanxes were fighting the main battle while the cavalry engaged in its own private skirmishes on the wings. Cavalry could also be used to attack light troops – slingers, peltasts and the like – as they could use their speed and manoeuvrability to ride down upon them. Infantry, particularly a hoplite phalanx, would rarely have made a direct attack against cavalry. In large part because it would have been a waste of effort for foot soldiers to charge at cavalry, since the mounted men could wheel out of the way before the infantry even came close, then, when the infantry became exhausted trying to catch them, turn back and ride down upon them.

Until the middle of the fourth century, cavalry and infantry acted separately from each other, for the most part. It was only in the late 360s, with the ascendancy of Macedonia and the reign of Philip II that the effectiveness of a combined infantry–cavalry attack was recognized.

Thessalian cavalryman with standard cavalry arms and armour, including the Boeotian-style helmet. (R. Baylis)

The perfection of the combined attack can be seen at the battle of Gaugamela where Alexander's attacking arm was composed of infantry and cavalry working in concert with each other to break through and cut down the Persian lines. With these combined attacks it is not always clear who these infantry were: in the case of Alexander they were usually the *hypaspists* (elite infantry), but elsewhere their identity is not always obvious. We do read of a unit of foot soldiers called the *hamippoi*, who are described as foot soldiers that fight in the ranks of the cavalry. These men were probably some form of light-armed infantry who were interspersed amongst the horses. Their role may have been to pull enemy cavalry off their horses and to dispatch them once they were on the ground. Cavalry were also essential in a pursuit, as they could cover a greater distance at a higher rate of speed than infantry. Thus, despite the greater expense associated with

Iron kopis. *This short sword was the preferred cavalry blade. (Metropolitan Museum of Art Open Content Program)*

maintaining a cavalry horse, it was nonetheless essential to the Greek army. As Xenophon succinctly puts it:

> ...suppose we have to fight: we have cavalry on our own side, but the enemy has a great many horsemen of outstanding ability. This means that if we win we will not be able to kill anyone, and if we lose we will not be able to save anyone. (Xenophon *Anabasis* 2.4)

A typical cavalryman wore a helmet, breastplate and high boots, but did not carry a shield. Xenophon dictated that the breastplate should be formed in a way that allowed the rider to sit comfortably on his horse whilst also having protective flaps on the lower edge to cover the rider's upper legs to some extent. For a helmet he gave clear preference to the Boeotian style, which essentially looked like a sunhat with its brim folded down. This helmet allowed the cavalryman the full range of his vision, while its sloping brim provided a fair degree of protection from missiles. As with the hoplite, the exact amount and type of armour worn by the cavalryman was often a personal preference and a reflection of wealth and status. For offensive arms the cavalryman carried either a single thrusting spear or two throwing javelins, as well as a sword, which was worn at the waist.

Xenophon preferred the style of the Persian cavalry blade, known as a *kopis*, with is single curved edge and tip heavy design. This made it ideal for striking downwards from horseback, particularly against infantry. As Xenophon points out, the cut of the *kopis* was far more useful than the thrust of a sword when fighting from a raised position.

Naval warfare

We associate the epic battles of ancient Greece with the land – Marathon, Thermopylae, Leuctra, Chaeronea – these battles were fought firmly on solid ground. We tend to, aside from Salamis, forget about the sea. Yet it was the sea that directed life in the Greek world. 'Hellas' did not just comprise the mainland Greek Peninsula, it was also an island culture, with hundreds of them scattered through the Aegean. The sea was central to life. Sparta may have marched to dominance on the rocky soil of the mainland, but the Athenians achieved similar power sailing the temperamental waters of the Mediterranean. For close to a century they were the uncontested masters of the sea. When in the closing years of the Peloponnesian war the Spartan Callicratidas boldly told the Athenian Conon 'I am going to stop your fornication with the sea. She belongs to me' (Xenophon *Hellenica* 1.6.15), he was not simply throwing threats around, he was asserting Sparta's claim to naval supremacy.

Ships and the sea were part of the Hellenic consciousness from the Bronze Age onwards. Piracy and raids were a part of regular life, and remained so even into the early 5th century. Raiding in particular was not seen as an act associated with lowlifes and criminals, rather, as an acceptable way to make a living. The men who sailed out on these raids rode on large penteconters: large galleys manned by 50 oarsmen.

These raiding ships were owned by wealthy individuals who were also responsible for gathering together crews. These crews were made up largely of friends, relatives, and volunteers who likely signed up in order to lay claim to a share of the profits from the raids. The significance of the sea is reflected in the increasing amount of influence accorded to the owners of these vessels, particularly with regards to politics and civic administration.

Chalcedony scaraboid: Vessel (probably a penteconter) with hoplites on board. (Metropolitan Museum of Art Open Content Program)

In exchange for this power they were each required to make at least one of their ships available for the state to use when a fleet was needed. Thus, the early Greek navies did not belong to the state, but to wealthy citizens who, as a result, came to control state policy and government. These fleets did not cost the state much, if anything; but the size of the fleet was rather limited.

As we have already seen the dramatic change in infantry warfare during the Archaic and early Classical periods was closely tied to the shifts in social organization, class designation etc. So too was the case with naval warfare. The hoplite symbolized the change on land, but at sea the great change came about in the shape of the trireme. The trireme was a long, sleek ship measuring 35m long, 6m wide and 3m high, with three tiers of oars, manned by 170 oarsmen. An additional 30 crew members brought the full complement of manpower on a trireme to 200, four times that of a penteconter which maxed out at 50 men. They were designed to serve as battleships, but could also be used to transport troops, as there was room on deck for an additional 30 passengers. Some

General design and construction of a trireme, showing the bottom bank of oars. There were an additional two rows above this. The sails would be taken down in battle. (R. Baylis)

triremes were modified to serve as horse transports to carry cavalry mounts. The trireme was aerodynamic and fast: when rowing at peak capacity a trireme could cross 130 nautical miles (240km) in a single day. The trireme seems to have been introduced to the Greek world via Persia, as the first Greek cities to make regular use of them were under Persian control.

Outside the Persian domain, triremes were privately owned, just as with the penteconters. However, they were considerably more expensive and time consuming to construct and so the penteconter remained the preferred vessel amongst the majority of private owners. Thus, if a state was keen to build up a fleet of triremes they could not rely on individuals, it would have to be done at state expense. The first state to do this was Corinth, they 'were the first to approach the modern style of naval architecture, and that Corinth was the first place in Hellas where *triremes* were built…' (Thucydides 1.13.2). As the tactical advantages of the trireme became apparent, the popularity of the ship began to spread. In some cases rival states competed fiercely to outdo their opponents in production levels – notably Athens and Aegina. By 480, the year the Persian king Xerxes invaded Greece, Athens had a whopping 200 triremes, outstripping all others with the size of their fleet. The navy was the first state owned military arm, and it was certainly a huge advantage to have a fleet at the ready, but it was also a massive financial burden. These ships were not crewed by volunteers, but by men hired and paid by the state. So who worked on these ships?

A trireme was headed by the trierarch. These men came from the wealthiest echelon of society. They did not necessarily have any previous naval experience, but they were rich. The trierarch's responsibility was to command and crew the ship assigned to him. He was also obliged to pay for the maintenance of the vessel, hence the necessary financial status. Exactly how much money he invested in the ship was up to the individual trierarch: some did the absolute bare minimum required to keep the vessel afloat, while others funded a complete overhaul to ensure theirs was the newest, sleekest, quickest trireme available. The crew of sailors was made up of a helmsman, a lookout, a rowing-master, shipwright, purser and 10 deckhands. As per standard practice, each trireme also carried 10 hoplites and 4 archers. It took a particular type of soldier to fight on a ship's deck as it heaved and rocked underneath them. The style of fighting required by these marines was far removed from that used by their colleagues on land. Finally, there were the oarsmen, the most essential part of the crew but also the lowest ranking. The three-tiered banks of oars – 62 on the top deck, 54 on the middle, and 54 on the bottom – were organized hierarchically based on social status. We do not know the percentage of slave vs. citizen oarsmen, but we can say with certainty that slave crews were always assigned to this lowest deck. Rowing was a brutal, physically demanding task; hence its frequent association with slavery, but in many cases large portions of the rowers were citizens. These were men who did not meet or have the financial means to serve as cavalry or hoplites, but on account of their citizen status could still serve in the army as oarsmen. Their low social status meant rowers were looked upon with disdain and they did not always have the most favourable reputation, even though they performed an essential civic service.

The fleet could be used to carry out a diverse range of functions – often performing several within the same campaign. We have already seen that triremes were often used to transport troops and horses. The most common task for the fleet was a throwback to the pre-Classical period: using ships to make raids on enemy coasts. This practice was particularly popular with the Athenians during the Peloponnesian war. These raids were meant to be lightening fast hit and run affairs with no pitched battles or lengthy campaigns, which meant it was not necessary to pack a large number of hoplites on board, allowing the ships to retain their speed and agility. A fleet could also be used to patrol sea routes, allowing them to control the movement of goods and supplies during times of war: Athens' control of the sea allowed her to bring in continual supplies throughout the Peloponnesian War even when under siege. The fleet could assist land forces during a siege by blockading the harbours of coastal cities, preventing allies from sending aid or assistance via the sea. Skirmishes were a common occurrence, far more so than an actual full scale pitched naval battle. When such an event did occur it involved just as much strategy as a land battle, with the instigators seeking to gain the upper hand over the opponents, even resorting to trickery at times, as Themistocles did at the battle of Salamis (see p.60). One of the most common tactics was to attack before the enemy ships were fully manned, as happened at Sphacteria, or while the crews were eating, typically during the midday meal: there was not much room on a trireme for supplies, so crews almost always had to put into land for food and water.

As with hoplite warfare, there was a pattern to how a naval battle worked. Each side would draw up into formation. If a fleet found itself considerably outnumbered they would form a circle with their prows facing out, to prevent themselves being flanked. However, the most common formation was a single line with the prows turned 90 degrees to form a column with the ships abreast of each other. It was rare for the ships to draw up in 2 or more lines: this increased the risk of a jam as the ships tried to manoeuvre, especially once damaged ships starting getting in the way. The ships had to be careful not to place themselves too close to each other within the formation as they ran the risk of becoming tangled up with each other. When battle commenced the ships would power forward under the strength of their oars, aiming to strike enemy triremes with the solid bronze rams on the prows of their ships. There were three manoeuvres that were essential to naval combat. The first two were closely connected, 'sailing through and out' and 'sailing round': a ship would push through the gap between two enemy vessels before wheeling about to ram one of them. The third was backing water or reversing to get clear of a rammed enemy ship. Once two ships came within range of each other, the marines on deck would spring into action, firing arrows and other missiles, and engaging in hand-to-hand combat once a ship had been boarded. In a way naval combat was an echo of single combat with each vessel picking out a suitable opponent and attacking them before moving on to another, rather than fighting as a massed, cohesive unit. A rammed trireme became disabled, but it did not sink because of its buoyancy. After a battle, the victor seized the damaged enemy ships and towed them away to repair them (if possible) and add them to their own fleet. The carnage experienced in a naval battle could be much greater than a land battle: in addition to the wreckage of broken or damaged ships clogging the waterways were the bodies of drowned men floating in the water as shipwrecked survivors struggled to swim to shore, being picked off by enemy boats or slaughtered by soldiers once they reached firm ground. For the oarsmen, particularly those on the lowest level, battle must have felt like a nightmare as they could not see anything of their surroundings trapped within the dark hold of the ship. Thucydides provides us with a vivid description of the chaos of a full scale naval combat when he writes of the final battle between the Syracusans and the Athenians in the Great Harbour:

> With many ships meeting in a small space (and this was a battle in a very small space between a very large number of ships – the combined total came to nearly 200), there was little direct ramming because of the lack of room to pull back for a charge through the line: more often there were accidental collisions, ship crashing into ship when attempting to escape or in pursuit of another. When one ship was bearing down on another, the men on the decks kept up a constant barrage of javelins, arrows, and stones: and when the two closed, the marines fought hand to hand in an effort to board the other. In many areas of the battle there was so little room that a ship which had rammed an enemy in one direction would find itself rammed from another, with the consequence that one ship would have two or sometimes even more ships entangled around it...And all the while the great din of so many ships crashing into one another both terrified the crews and made it impossible for them to hear the orders shouted by the coxswains – and indeed on both sides they were shouting loud, not only technical directions but also encouragement of the immediate struggle for victory. (Thucydides 7.70.4–7).

735	First Messenian War
670	Second Messenian War
650	The reforms of Lycurgus in Sparta
499	Persians attack Naxos; Aristagoras travels to Greece
498	Athenians, Eretrians, and Ionians attack Sardis
490	Battle of Marathon
480	Battles of Thermopylae and Salamis
479	Battle of Plataea
478/7	Formation of the Delian League
466	Battle of the Eurymedon
462	Spartans appeal for aid against the revolt at Ithome
451	5-year truce between Athens and Sparta, 50-year truce between Sparta and Argos
449	Peace of Callias between Athens and Persis
446	30 Years' Peace between Athens and Sparta
433	Alliance between Athens and Corcyra
432	Revolt of Potidaea; Megarian Decree
431	Spartans invade Attica
430	Plague in Athens
428/7	Mytilene revolt
425	Athenian's fortify Pylos, capture the Spartans on Sphacteria
424	Amphipolis taken by the Spartans
421	Peace of Nicias
418	Battle of Mantinea
416	Athenians take Melos
415–413	Athenian expedition to Sicily

405	Athenians defeated at Aegospotami
401	March of the ten thousand
394–387/6	Corinthian War
371	Battle of Leuctra
359	Philip II becomes king of Macedon
353	Battle of the Crocus Field
338	Battle of Chaeronea
336	Alexander the Great becomes king of Macedon
335	Destruction of Thebes
334	Battle of the Granicus
333	Battle of Issus
331	Battle of Gaugamela
326	Battle of the Hydaspes
323	Death of Alexander the Great

Periods of Greek History

3000–1000: Bronze Age
1000–750: Dark Ages
750–480: Archaic Period
480–323: Classical Period
323–31/30: Hellenistic Period

CHAPTER 1

THE PERSIAN WARS

THE SERIES OF BATTLES COMMONLY KNOWN as the Persian Wars hold a central position in the western psyche. Traditionally viewed as an iconic clash between east and west they are depicted as the triumph of the independent, stubborn Greeks against Persian (foreign) tyranny and imperialism. It was a watershed moment in western history when the 'little guy' stood up to the 'big guy' and against all odds won out. One of the most common sentiments about the outcome of the Persian Wars is that the Greek victory prevented the orientalization of the west; in other words, the notion that had the Greeks lost the entire development of western civilization would have altered and our world would look rather different today. This might be a bit of an exaggeration, but we cannot discount the fact that the Persian Wars were very much a formative moment in the Hellenic world. The Persian Wars are also unique in that they were the first in western history to be recorded in a detailed manner from an investigative or empirical point of view. This is entirely thanks to an ambitious individual – Herodotus of Halicarnassus – who wrote his very significant text *The Histories* in the 5th century BC a few decades after the Wars. The term 'history' means an inquiry, and that is exactly what *The Histories* is – a detailed investigation into the causes of and events of the Persian War. Herodotus' text does not simply provide a record of historical events, the author goes beyond that, analyzing events, seeking explanations and speaking with eyewitnesses to try and create a comprehensive account. On account of this, Herodotus is known as the 'Father of History' and *The Histories* is intrinsic to any study of the period.

The Ionian revolt

The Persian Wars were by no means the first contact between the Greek world and Persia. The west coast of Asia Minor (modern day Turkey) was home to a large number of Greek cities (the Ionian Greeks): Halicarnassus, the hometown of Herodotus, was one of them. These cities had been under Persian control for some time – essentially from the foundation of the Persian Empire in the 6th century BC by Cyrus the Great, the first Achaemenid king. Several of the eastern Greek Aegean islands also fell under Persian control – notably Lesbos, Chios, and Samos. Greeks inhabited these cities and islands, but they were

The **Persian Empire/Achaemenid dynasty** was founded by Cyrus the Great who took the throne of a small Persian territory in 550. He subsequently conquered the territories of Media, Sardis, Lydia, Babylonia, and parts of Central Asia, laying the foundation for what would become the largest land empire known at that time. At its height the Persian Empire stretched from Egypt to the Indus. This vast expanse of territory was home to millions of people from many cultures and religions, all ruled by a single king via a centralized administration under a unified political structure.

governed by a Persian satrap and were required to pay tribute to the king. The Persians were relatively tolerant overlords. If the city paid tribute and did what was expected of it, they were essentially left to their own devices; if they did not, well, then things could get a little difficult for them. It was within these cities and islands of the Persian Empire that the seeds of conflict between Greece and Persia were planted.

The Greco-Persian conflict did not come out of nowhere, and though its development is due in large part to rebellion among the Greeks of Asia Minor, we cannot discount the role played by Persian imperialistic tendencies – expanding the empire west towards Greece was a logical next step. In 499, the Persians indicated this by sending a fleet against the island of Naxos, situated in the Cyclades. Control of Naxos would have given the Persians a very strategic jumping off point for further movement towards mainland Greece. Despite being caught unawares, the Naxians, were not keen to submit to Persian rule.

Although outnumbered, they stubbornly held out against their attackers for four months, at which point the Persians gave up and withdrew 'when all the supplies they had brought on the expedition had been exhausted' (Herodotus 5.34.2). The resiliency of the Naxians gave Persia a taste of Greek independence, a theme that will be ongoing throughout this chapter.

By choosing to withdraw their fleet from Naxos without achieving even a semblance of a victory, the Persians made themselves vulnerable as they had indicated weakness, never a good idea when trying to maintain authority over a vast and diverse empire. This provided the impetus for the beginnings of rebellion in Asia Minor, spearheaded by Aristagoras, the tyrant of Miletus. The exact cause of his decision is unclear, but it was likely related to the failed Persian attack on Naxos that Aristagoras had played a significant part in instigating. Regardless, Aristagoras gave up his position as tyrant and became the leader of the Ionian independence movement. Aristagoras' inflammatory rhetoric had an immediate impact on

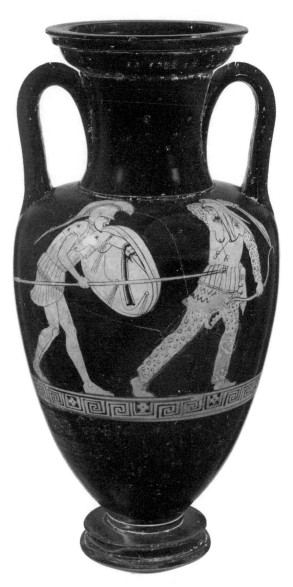

*Red Figure Amphora. Battle between a Greek hoplite and a Persian archer.
The Persians were renowned for their archery skills. (Metropolitan Museum
of Art Open Content Program)*

the other Ionian cities, many of which became eager to throw off the Persian yoke.

Despite their enthusiasm for the cause, these cities inherently understood that they could not manage this feat alone, as they were vastly outnumbered with regards to both resources and manpower. Thus, they turned to mainland Greece for help. The Ionians felt that the logical starting point was Sparta: after all, if one was going to seek military aid, why not go straight to the preeminent military power. Aristagoras made the trek to Sparta where he pitched his case for the liberation of the Ionian Greeks to king Cleomenes. It seemed that things were going in his favour and he was winning the Spartans over, until the moment when they realized where exactly Aristagoras was asking them to go.

> When the day they had appointed for the answer arrived and they met at the place they had agreed upon, Cleomenes asked Aristagoras how many days the journey would take to go from the sea of the Ionians to the King. Aristagoras, though he had cleverly misled Cleomenes in everything else, stumbled at this point. For he ought not to have told him the real distance if he wanted to bring the Spartans into Asia, but instead, he told them it was a journey of three months inland. (Herodotus 5.50.1–2)

Tyranny was one of many political systems that existed in the Greek world. The term 'tyrant' was not considered pejorative in antiquity. Tyrants often came to power during periods of prolonged civil discord. The first generation of their rule brought stability and prosperity to city-states, often through public works programs; however, things tended to turn south with the second generation of rule as the ruler became increasingly autocratic.

Such a journey was inconceivable for the perpetually inward-looking Spartans. Fearing a Helot revolt should they travel too far from home, the Spartans sent Aristagoras packing, saying 'My guest-friend of Miletus, you must depart from Sparta before sunset. Your request will never be accepted by the Lacedaemonians if you intend to lead them on a three-month journey away from the sea' (Herodotus 5.50.3). Aristagoras was not yet prepared to accept this rejection: instead of departing he went to plead directly with Cleomenes at his house. Before he could present his case anew, Cleomenes' daughter, Gorgo (who was only 8 or 9 at the time) interjected:

> Father, this miserable little foreigner will ruin you completely unless you drive him out of the house pretty quick. (Plutarch *Sayings of Spartan Women* Gorgo.1)

Cleomenes heeded this advice and refused to speak any further with Aristagoras.

Aristagoras' next stop was Argos, a long-standing rival of Sparta. Perhaps he hoped that they would be willing to do what the Spartans had refused simply to spite them. Unfortunately, the Argives too refused the Ionian cause. It is a strong possibility that their decision was controlled in large part by a recently received oracle from Delphi, which prophesied doom and gloom for the Argives if they became embroiled in Milesian affairs. Finally, Aristagoras made his way to Athens where he managed to secure a promise of aid from both the Athenians and the Eretrians (a large city on the island of Euboea). Why the Athenians and Eretrians agreed to support the revolt when several other major states had refused is not entirely clear. The Athenians did have a bit of a pre-existing chip on their shoulders with regards to the Persians, as they were housing the recently ousted Athenian tyrant, Hippias, who no doubt had his eye on regaining his former position with the help of the Persians. As Herodotus writes:

It was just at this juncture, when they were feeling quite antagonistic toward the Persians, that Aristagoras of Miletus arrived in Athens after his expulsion from Sparta by Cleomenes of Lacedaemon. For after Sparta, Athens was the next most powerful state. When Aristagoras appeared before the Athenian people, he repeated the same things that he had said in Sparta about the good things in Asia and about Persian warfare – that they used neither shields nor spears and how easy it would be to subdue them. In addition, he told them that Miletus was originally an Athenian colony, and therefore, since the Athenians were a great power, it was only fair and reasonable for them to offer protection to the Milesians. There was nothing he failed to promise them, since he was now in dire need, and at last he managed to win them over. (Herodotus 5.97.1–2)

As for the Eretrians, they reportedly agreed to join 'in order to repay a debt they owed to the Milesians…' (Herodotus 5.99.1). Yet, there must have been more to their decision. On the one hand, they clearly realized that the Persians would not look upon the Ionian revolt favourably, nor would they turn a blind eye to those who supported it. They must have, even to a minor degree, considered the fact that the Persians would eventually look west towards Greece to expand their already sizeable empire. It also appears that Aristagoras downplayed the size and strength of the Persian army, and for some reason the Athenians and Eretrians believed him, which is rather remarkable when you consider the sheer size of the Persian Empire, much of which had been gained through conquest. Nonetheless, Aristagoras' words worked and the Athenians and Eretrians both agreed to send ships to support the Ionians, 20 and 5 respectively.

In 498 the Athenian and Eretrian ships met up with a primarily Milesian force at the Ionian city of Ephesus, from whence they marched inland to attack the provincial capital of Sardis, which 'they captured…without resistance from anyone whatsoever' (Herodotus 5.100.1). The satrap of Sardis, Artaphernes, was caught entirely unawares but managed to hold off his attackers by maintaining control of the acropolis, which he defended with a large force. The arrival of Persian reinforcements placed the invaders in a vulnerable position, and so they made a hasty retreat to Ephesus having accomplished very little other than burning a portion of the city and angering the Persians. The retreating Greek force was overtaken just outside of Ephesus and suffered heavy losses. The surviving Athenian and Eretrians limped home with news of their defeat and the realization that the Persian army described by Aristagoras and the Persian army in reality were two very different things. They washed their hands of the situation 'and although Aristagoras sent many messengers with appeals to the Athenians, they refused to help the Ionians any further' (Herodotus 5.103.1).

The involvement of these two Greek cities in the attack on Sardis did not go unnoticed by the Persian king, Darius I. He vowed to strike back, indeed 'he appointed one of his attendants to repeat to him three times whenever dinner was served: "My lord, remember the Athenians"' (Herodotus 5.105.2).

For the moment he was forced to be patient in his desire for revenge due to the ongoing actions of the Ionians who, despite the debacle at Sardis, were not prepared to give up. Instead they moved to spread the rebellion north towards the Hellespont and south to Caria. At the same time, they offered support to the island of Cyprus, which had rebelled against Persia. Darius was forced to focus his attention on quashing the rebellions in Asia Minor and the Eastern Aegean islands, which he did efficiently and systematically. Finally, in 494 he was able to focus on the heart of the rebellion – Miletus. By this point the Milesians had tired of Aristagoras, but his death in battle against the Thracians left the Milesians at a bit of a loss with regards to how they should proceed. Along with their remaining allies, they made a determined effort to resist the Persian assault on their city, but the absence of unified leadership led to the desertion of several allies and their ships, leaving Miletus without a fleet to protect it. Meanwhile, the Persians were taking advantage of the vast network of resources available to them to besiege Miletus. Bit by bit all of the cities and islands that had joined in Aristagoras' rebellion were subdued and punished harshly, particularly Miletus. According to Herodotus the fall of Miletus had been predicted by the oracle at Delphi, but in a strange turn of events, the prophecy was not uttered to Milesian envoys, but rather to an Argive group: the same oracle that prophesied trouble for Argos should they involve themselves with Miletus also gave a second response:

> The time will come, Milesians, devisers of evil deeds,
>> When many will feast on you: a splendid gift for them;
>> Your wives will wash the feet of many long-haired men,
>> And others will assume the care of my own temple at Didyma
> (Herodotus 6.19.2)

The oracle's predictions proved true: the temple of Apollo at Didyma fell to the Persians and the Milesian women found themselves enslaved to 'long-haired men'– the Persians. With the Ionian revolt brought to a close, Darius could now turn his attention farther west, looking beyond the Cycladic islands to mainland Greece. In 492 Darius made his move by appointing his relative, Mardonius, commander of the Ionian region and sending him into Thrace and along the northern Aegean towards Macedonia to begin paving the way for a Persian invasion of Greece.

The battle of Marathon

Things really kicked off in 491 when Darius sent envoys to several major Greek cities demanding they submit to Persian authority by giving him the symbolic gifts of earth and water.

Darius' demands received mixed responses: all the island states capitulated as did several on the mainland (they 'medized'– joined the Medes/Persians), but others reacted with anger. The Athenians in particular went so far as to throw the envoys into a well. Their excessive reaction to the envoy's request may have been connected to the ongoing presence of Hippias in Persia. With his demands soundly rejected by the Athenians, on whom he had sworn vengeance, Darius called up an army, which was made up of levies from across the Persian Empire and prepared to sail for Greece under the command of Datis, while Darius himself remained in Persia. The purpose of this expedition does not appear to have been a large-scale conquest, but rather to secure a foothold in eastern Greece, which the Persians could use as a base for campaigns further inland. It also had the underlying purpose of punishing the Eretrians and Athenians for their role in the Ionian revolt. The Persian fleet did not make a beeline for the mainland, but sailed via several of the islands, starting with Naxos, all of which submitted, thereby securing a supply line across the Aegean between Persia and Greece. From there the Persian fleet made for Eretrian territory on Euboea. The Eretrians, realising that they were outnumbered:

> …had no intention of marching out to meet them in battle, so now their prevailing plan was to stay in the city, and their main concern was to defend its walls if they possibly could. The assault on the walls was fierce and lasted for six days, and many fell on both sides. On the seventh day, two prominent citizens, Euphorbus son of Alcimachus and Philagrus son of Cyneas, betrayed their city and surrendered it to the Persians. After entering the city, the Persians plundered and set fire to the sanctuaries, exacting vengeance for the sanctuaries burned down in Sardis, and as Darius had instructed, they enslaved the people. (Herodotus 6.101.2–3).

The Persian fleet then turned their attention towards Athenians and their homeland of Attica. On the advice of Hippias, they made for the plain of Marathon, a place that provided ideal terrain for the Persians as it would allow them to make use of both their larger numbers as well as their cavalry, the bulwark of the Persian army.

The Athenians had not remained idle. They had gathered together 6,000 hoplites as well as 600 Plataean allies before marching to meet the Persians at Marathon. There was a noted absence of Spartan hoplites at Marathon: they had agreed to send a small force to help, but were unable to set out immediately as they were in the middle of a major religious festival which made it 'impossible for them to do so at that moment, since they did not wish to break their law. For that day was the ninth of the month, and on the ninth, they said, they could not march out to war, but must instead wait until the moon was full' (Herodotus 6.106.3). Thus, the Greeks who met the Persians at Marathon were considerably outnumbered.

Upon arriving at Marathon, the 10 Athenian generals found themselves in a stalemate with regards to their course of action: some preferred to sit tight and await a Persian advance, while other pushed to attack immediately in the hopes of catching the enemy unawares. The vote was split evenly with five generals being pro-battle, and five against. The polemarch, Callimachus, was charged with casting the deciding vote. Militades, who was in the pro-war camp, took the initiative and said to Callimachus:

> It is now up to you, Callimachus, whether you will reduce Athens to slavery or ensure its freedom and thus leave to all posterity a memorial for yourself... For from the time Athenians first came into existence up until the present, this is the greatest danger they have ever confronted. If they bow down before the Medes [another name for the Persians], it is clear from our past experience what they will suffer when handed over to Hippias; but if this city prevails, it can become the first among all Greek cities... If we fail to fight now, I expect that intense factional strife will fall upon the Athenians and shake their resolve so violently that they will medise. But if we join battle before any rot can infect some of the Athenians, then, as long as the gods grant both sides equal treatment, we can prevail in this engagement. All this is now in your hands and depends on you. If you add your vote for my proposal, your ancestral land can be free and your city the first of Greek cities. But if you choose the side of those eager to prevent a battle, you will have the opposite of all the good things I have described. (Herodotus 6.109.3–6)

Red Figure Kylix. Running hoplites. Note the different devices painted on their shields. (Walters Art Museum Open Content Program)

Militades proved persuasive. Callimachus voted in favour of attack, and Militades was put in charge. The Greeks made their move early in the day. In accordance with tradition, Callimachus as polemarch was stationed on the right wing, then the ten tribes (each representing one hoplite unit) were stationed one next to the other. Finally, the Plataeans were posted on the far left wing. The Greeks were well aware of the fact that they were at a significant disadvantage numerically and so were forced to spread their lines quite thin to avoid the risk of being outflanked. 'The result of the Athenians' deployment at Marathon was that the line of the Athenian army was equal in length to that of the Medes, but the center of the Athenian line was only a few rows deep and thus the army was at its weakest there…' (Herodotus 6.111.3). Moreover, the Greek force was made up primarily of hoplites, while that of the Persians was considerably more diverse with slingers, archers and javelin men in addition to heavy infantry and cavalry. These lightly armed soldiers could attack the hoplites from a distance, cutting down their numbers before they even reached the front of the Persian lines.

The burial mound for the Greek dead at Marathon. (J. Butera)

To counter this, the Greeks chose to use speed and surprise as their strategy. The reasoning behind this seems to have been an attempt to avoid being completely mowed down by missiles, with the added effect of startling the Persians. Herodotus tells us that:

> …when the Athenians were let loose and allowed to advance, they charged at a run toward the barbarians…and the Persians who saw the Athenians advancing towards them on the double, prepared to meet the attack; they assumed that the Athenians were seized by some utterly self-destructive madness, as they observed how few the Athenians were in number and how they were charging towards them with neither cavalry nor archers in support… but when the Athenians closed with them in combat, they fought remarkably well. For they were the first of all Hellenes we know of to use the running charge against their enemies… (Herodotus 6.113.1–3).

In keeping with tradition, the Persians had stationed their strongest fighters at the center of the line, and these men were able to repel the initial Greek charge. The Greeks, however, had massed the strongest parts of the Athenian and Plataean forces on the wings, even though it weakened their center. These men were able to put pressure on the Persian flanks, enveloping them and breaking the cohesion of the Persian line. The Persian wings collapsed in on themselves, at which point Persian resistance crumbled. The Persians turned and fled back towards their camp. It was only the discipline of the Persian officers that prevented a total rout as they managed to stay coolheaded and organized enough to get a number of their men back onto the ships while the Athenians 'pursued them and cut them down until the reached the sea, where they called for a fire and started to seize the ships' (Herodotus 6.113.2). The battle at Marathon had ended an entirely unexpected defeat for the Persians who, according to the sources (and we must always leave room for bias here) lost 6,400 men. The Athenians are said to have lost only 192. The Athenian dead were cremated and buried in a funeral mound on the battlefield, which can still be seen today. The Spartans, true to their world, did send a force of 2,000 hoplites to Marathon as soon as they were able to, but they arrived a day too late.

Marathon was a watershed moment for the Greeks, particularly the Athenians. They had withstood the army of a barbarian invader, one that both vastly outnumbered them and had a history of successful foreign conquest. The Athenians had proven their bravery and ability on the battlefield, their mettle

Phidippides is a figure closely tied to the lore of Marathon. There are two stories associated with this name. The first reports that he ran from Athens to Sparta (c. 240km) in a day to request Spartan aid at Marathon. The second is that he ran from Marathon to Athens (c. 40km) bearing the news of the Greek victory. It is this run that serves as the template for our modern marathons.

as hoplites, a reputation generally reserved for the Spartans. The Persians, on the other hand, had once again received a taste of Greek stubbornness and their refusal to submit to imperial authority/autocracy. The puzzling thing about the battle of Marathon is the apparent absence of the Persian cavalry: Herodotus makes no reference to them. This is rather odd as the flower of the Persian army was their cavalry, and this gave them a distinct advantage over the Greeks at Marathon who were lacking horsemen. Moreover, the terrain at Marathon was ideal for cavalry deployment. After the battle their fleet set sail for Athens, it seems they had expected certain individuals to betray the city to them, or so the story goes. When this did not happen, and they realized they would not be able to force their way in, they turned and sailed for home. Despite their defeat, the Persians were not prepared to give up. Marathon may have been embarrassing, particularly following the headache of the Ionian revolt, but it did not steer Darius from his desire to put the Greeks in their place.

Herodotus states that Darius was absolutely infuriated by the Greek victory at Marathon, refusing to forget the insult and vowed to have his revenge, for he 'had already been thoroughly exasperated by the Athenians' attack on Sardis, he now reacted with a much more intense fury and became even more determined to make war on Hellas than he had before' (Herodotus 7.1.1). He began by drawing up the levies from across the empire, to amass an army considerably larger than the one he had sent to Marathon. Unfortunately for Darius, he died before he could see this expedition brought to fruition. Thus, the mantle of revenge fell to his son and heir, Xerxes, who was reluctant to take on his father's quest. However, Mardonius made it his mission to pester Xerxes until he changed his mind, telling him things like 'My lord, it is unreasonable that the Athenians have inflicted great evils upon the Persians but have paid no penalty for it…you must march against Athens in order to gain a good reputation among men and to ensure that others will beware of making war on your land afterward' (Herodotus 7.5.2).

Xerxes' invasion

Xerxes' invasion of Greece was no small affair: the conquest of Greece became the focal point of his reign, particularly as the first years of his kingship had been spent putting down rebellions in various parts of the empire. He had to prove that he was a strong and competent ruler, and he intended to use Greece to make this point. The army that marched on and sailed to Greece was a direct reflection of the power and extent of Persian rule. In 481 Xerxes moved to Sardis and began gathering the army, while also dealing with the logistical aspects of his upcoming expedition. Herodotus provides us with a detailed list of the various ethnic components of the army (7.61–99). His numbers are a bit problematic, as they place the size of the army at 1.8 million, with an additional 2.6 million non-military members. These numbers are no doubt an exaggeration but we can be sure that Xerxes' army was huge; far larger than anything the Greeks were able to field, both on land and at sea. The sheer logistics of moving this army were astonishing, especially with regards to finding or transporting food and water.

The planning that went into this expedition is indicative of how seriously Xerxes viewed the conquest of Greece. Amongst his personal retainers was Demaratus, an exiled Spartan king who would act as an advisor for Xerxes, particularly with regards to the traditions and customs of the Spartans. Xerxes himself was baffled by the notion that any of the Greeks would risk opposing his army given how outnumbered they were sure to be. When asked outright by Xerxes whether the Greeks would fight, and if so, why on earth they would chose to do so, Demaratus' response was thus 'in Hellas, poverty is always and forever a native resident, while excellence is something acquired through intelligence and the force of strict law. It is through the exercise of this excellence that Hellas wards off both poverty and despotism' (Herodotus 7.102.1). In other words, Greek resistance would very much be an issue for Xerxes. With regards to the fighting

Achaemenid relief: A Persian guard – the top of his ornate but effective bow is visible. (Metropolitan Museum of Art Open Content Program)

power of the Greeks, Demaratus focused on the Spartans and he informed Xerxes:

> The Lacedaemonians are in fact no worse than any other man when they fight individually, but when they unite and fight together, the are the best warriors of all. For though they are free, they are not free in all respects, for they are actually ruled by a lord and master: law is their master, and it is the law that they inwardly fear – much more so than your men fear you. They do whatever it commands, which is always the same: it forbids them to flee from battle, and no matter how many men they are fighting, it orders them to remain in their rank and either prevail or perish. (Herodotus 7.104.4–5)

The news that a very large foreign army was making for Greek shores caused mixed reactions: some cities came together in a coalition known as the Hellenic League. The member states agreed to the unprecedented act of putting aside their own personal disputes for the greater cause of dealing with Persia. Sparta was given control of both land and sea operations, although the suggestion was made that Athens should be given control of the naval forces, but the League ultimately decided that having two different states in charge of different military arms would lead to complications. Not every city was keen to join the League. Many, especially those in northern Greece, opened their gates to the Persians and medized, allowing them unimpeded passage through their territories. Although there were sound strategic reasons for their decisions, the choice to medize rather than resist the Persians would be held against them for generations to come.

Within the Hellenic League, however, things were not exactly smooth sailing. The member states were divided over the question of where they should make their stand against the Persians. The Peloponnesians pushed for fortifying the Isthmus of Corinth. From a strategic viewpoint, this was not an unreasonable suggestion, as the narrow Isthmus would be a straightforward place to blockade with a relatively small number of soldiers; but such an action would leave all the territory north of the Isthmus, including Athens, vulnerable. After much debate, the League finally agreed upon a place to face the Persians. They chose a spot in central Greece, the only route through which Xerxes' army could march south, a narrow pass known as the 'Hot Gates': Thermopylae. Herodotus tells us that 'The Hellenes planned to defend this pass in an attempt to keep the barbarian out of Hellas, and also to have their fleet sail to Artemision… so that their land and sea forces would be close…' (Herodotus 7.175.2). The exact location – the middle gate at Thermopylae – had been chosen for its strategic advantage. It was bordered by steep mountains on one side and the sea on the other, while the narrow strip of land that made up the pass was only 15 meters wide. Thus, the Persian advantage of considerably larger numbers would be negated, as would the abilities of the Persian cavalry. The pass also had the remains of a defensive wall, which the Greeks immediately set about rebuilding once they arrived.

The battles of Thermopylae and Artemision

The battle of Thermopylae is without a doubt one of the most famous in western history. It was the first stand of the vastly outnumbered Greeks, led by the indomitable three hundred Spartans. While the three hundred are indeed an important part of the story, there was far more to Thermopylae. In fact, the army that marched to Thermopylae was only slightly smaller than that which faced off with the Persians at Marathon, numbering at around 8,000 hoplites from the League states, with the bulk of them coming from central Greece. Several Arcadian city states were also represented in the Peloponnesian contingent, contributing around 2,800 men. Alongside the Spartans were their helot attendants, who could also fight as light armed infantry, as well as approximately 1,000 other Laconian hoplites, primarily members of the *perioikoi* (non-Spartan inhabitants of Laconia).

Why were the numbers from the Peloponnese so paltry, particularly from Sparta, when compared to those contributed by central Greece? Herodotus provides us with two reasons: prohibitions resulting from religious festivals, and the celebration of the Olympic Games. In addition to this land force was a fleet of 271 triremes, provided primarily by Athens, Aegina and Corinth. This fleet stationed itself at Artemision off the coast of Euboea, not far from Thermopylae. The infantry was lead by the Spartan king, Leonidas, while the fleet was under the command of another Spartan.

Although Thermopylae is remembered as an infantry battle, it also coincides with key naval events. Immediately after

Thermopylae was chosen as the place to make a stand the oracle at Delphi was consulted for advice, it told the Hellenes 'to pray to the winds, because they would prove to be good allies of Hellas' (Herodotus 7.178.1); and indeed, the winds did choose to favour the Greeks as Xerxes' fleet was to find out on several consecutive occasions. While anchored at Magnesia en route to Thermopylae a sudden storm blew in. As a result of this storm 'no fewer than 400 ships were destroyed, and that it was impossible to count the men or estimate the immense quantity of material goods lost' (Herodotus 7.190.1). He then lost additional ships in the naval battle at Artemision, where the lighter, more nimble Greek vessels proved their worth against the much larger Persian fleet, capturing 45 enemy ships in total: 15 prior to the start of battle and 30 in the course of the fighting.

The Greek fleet achieved this victory despite being vastly outnumbered and in a weaker position:

> When Xerxes' soldiers and commanders saw the Hellenes sailing at them in their few ships, they assumed they were utterly mad. They now brought their own ships out to sea, expecting to capture the Greek ships easily, which was a very reasonable expectation, as they could see that the Hellenes had only a small number of ships and that they had many times more, and that their own were in better sailing condition, too. So it was with pride and contempt that they surrounded the Hellenes in a circle of their ships...When the Hellenes got the signal, the first thing they did was to turn the prows of their ships outward to face the barbarians, drawing their sterns close together toward a central point. At the second signal, they applied themselves to the work at hand, though hemmed within a confined space and facing the enemy ships head on. In the battle that ensued, they took thirty of the barbarians' ships... (Herodotus 8.11.1–2)

Finally, Persian naval luck continued to decline when another storm caught 200 Persian ships, seriously depleting the strength of the fleet, an act which Herodotus considers 'the god's doing, so that the Persian side would be equal to instead of much greater than the Greek side' (Herodotus 8.13.1). The victory at Artemision did much to boost Greek naval confidence, encouraging them to take offensive action. This boost in morale would serve them well at the upcoming battle of Salamis. The arrival of an additional 53 triremes from Athens had the bonus effect of helping to level out the numbers.

Back on land, Leonidas was coming to grips with the task set before him. Upon seeing the sheer size of Xerxes' army he immediately sent for reinforcements. According to Herodotus, Xerxes was utterly disdainful of what he viewed to be a paltry Greek army, believing that he would gain a quick and easy victory, he could not believe 'that the Lacedaemonians were really preparing to kill or be killed, to fight as much as was in their power, seemed to him to be the height of folly, the action of fools' (Herodotus 7.209.1). Convinced that the Greeks would lose heart and flee once they realized just how outnumbered they were, Xerxes contented himself with waiting. After five days he realized that the defenders were not going anywhere, but 'were instead holding their positions in what seemed to him a display of reckless impudence, he lost his temper and ordered the Medes and the Cissians out against them' (Herodotus 7.210.1). The defenders had chosen their location well, though. The combination of terrain and Greek tenacity proved a formidable obstacle for the Persians, as the infantry Xerxes had ordered forwards soon discovered. 'The Medes charged headlong into the Hellenes and great numbers of them fell. Although others rushed forth to replace them, even they could not drive the Hellenes away... Indeed, the Hellenes made it clear to everyone, and especially to the King himself, that although there were many in his army, there were few real men' (Herodotus 7.210.2). Xerxes then sent out his elite infantry, the Immortals. He had every expectation that they would succeed where the previous detachments had failed, but 'they fared no better than the Medes, and indeed they suffered the very same setbacks' (Herodotus 7.211.1). The confined space of the pass meant the Greeks did not have to send as many troops to the front line, allowing them

Red figure kylix: Hoplite with his equipment, attended by a young boy; it was common for hoplites to bring attendants to battle. (Metropolitan Museum of Art Open Content Program)

to work in shifts, with recovery periods in between, with the result that the Persians suffered heavy losses during the first days of engagement. Xerxes had anticipated an easy victory, but was instead fighting a war of attrition, in which he was losing far larger numbers of men than his opponents. Things turned in Xerxes' favour in the form of a local by the name of Ephialtes, who offered to betray the Greeks by leading a detachment of Persians around the Greeks via a mountain path so they could outflank the defenders and attack them from the rear. This task was entrusted to his elite infantry, the Immortals. En route they encountered a detachment of 1,000 Phocians whom Leonidas had placed along the path as a safeguard. When they spotted the Persians these troops took up a defensive position on the higher ground and prepared to fight; the Persians were caught entirely unawares at the sight of these men. The Phocians were prepared to defend their post to the death, but after firing an initial volley of arrows the Persians hurried onwards to deal with the main body of Greeks. This allowed a few Phocian scouts to make for Leonidas to appraise him of the situation, giving him a precious few hours to prepare for the coming onslaught which would see his troops pinned between two halves of Xerxes' army. Leonidas was no fool: he knew that this was a death sentence. And so, he appears to have made the decision to send away the bulk of the Greeks, as it was senseless to waste the manpower. Only 300 Spartans, 400 Thebans, and 700 Thespians remained. The Thebans had hoped to leave, but Leonidas mistrusted them, particularly as their city had already medized, and so he forced them to stay in what was essentially a hostage capacity. A message was dispatched to the fleet at Artemision to warn them that the invaders would soon be clear of the pass and moving into central Greece.

Leonidas and his men did not give up the pass without a serious fight, and large numbers of Persians were killed when they encountered the ferocious Greek defence who refused to give ground so long as they lived. Herodotus provides us with a vivid description of the ensuing battle:

> Many of the barbarians fell, for the leaders of the regiments were behind them with whips, flogging each and every man and urging them ever forward. Many fell into the sea and died, but ever more were trampled alive by one another. There was no counting the number of dead. The Hellenes knew they were about to face death at the hands of the men who had come around the mountain, and so they exerted their utmost strength against the barbarians, with reckless desperation and no regard for their own lives.
>
> By this time most of their spears had broken, so they were killing the Persians with their swords. And it was during this struggle that Leonidas fell, the man who had proved himself the most valiant of all, and with him those other famous Spartans... (Herodotus 7.223.3–224.1)

The death of Leonidas did little to sway the defenders, though they were now without a leader. Instead of submitting, the remaining few (except for the Thebans, who had indeed betrayed them) regrouped on a small hill and 'tried to defend themselves with their daggers if they still had them, or if not, with their hands and their teeth' (Herodotus 7.225.3). Only a hail of Persian arrows managed to finally bring them down. The resilience and defiance of the Greek defenders infuriated Xerxes, even in victory. If we are to believe Herodotus' numbers, the Greek resistance had cost Xerxes 20,000 men. Even if these numbers are exaggerated, Xerxes was no doubt astounded by the bizarre behaviour of the Greeks, who had chosen death over Persian rule. Indeed, the attitude of the Greeks towards the invaders and the utter irreverence for their numbers is best summed up by the famous anecdote about the Spartan Dieneces:

> It is reported that before the Hellenes engaged the Medes in battle, one of the Trachinians said that there were so many barbarians that whenever they shot their arrows, the sun was blocked by their number. Dieneces was not alarmed to hear this but rather, in total disregard for the vast numbers of Medes, said that what his Trachinian friend had reported was in fact good news, since it meant that while the Medes were blocking the sun, they would fight them in the shade. (Herodotus 7.226.1-2)

Herodotus tells us that Xerxes enslaved and branded the Theban troops, even though their city had surrendered to him, and he had the corpse of Leonidas decapitated.

Why did Leonidas and his men stay and engage in a final battle that guaranteed death? We know that the Greeks, and particularly the Spartans, were superstitious. Herodotus mentions a prophecy from the oracle at Delphi, which declared that a Spartan king had to die to prevent the city from falling to the Persians.

> As for you who dwell in the vast land of Sparta,
>> Either your city of glory will perish, sacked by the Perseids,

The modern monument at Thermopylae. Even today it remains one of the most famous battles in western history. (J. Butera)

> Or else the boundaries of Lacedaemon will grieve for the death of a king born of Heracles,
> Since neither bulls nor lions have enough might
> To oppose him, for the power of Zeus is in his possession.
> And he, I declare, will not be restrained until one or the other is torn apart. (Herodotus 7.220.3)

Perhaps the Spartans also wanted to prove that they were committed to the cause, as did the other troops who stayed? Maybe they wanted to make a clear statement to Xerxes that, although the city states of northern Greece had opened their gates to him, the members of the Hellenic League were determined to fight tooth and nail for their freedom, that the conquest of Greece would be far from a cakewalk for him.

Thermopylae had a significant impact on the Greek psyche: although the land battle had ended in defeat, their fleet had gained confidence at sea. Moreover, it represented a moral victory, a staunch refusal to sacrifice the Greek ideals of independence.

Those who fell in defence of Greece were honoured with an epitaph erected at the site of the battle, composed by the poet Simonides. Although the monument contains several verses, the most famous refers to the Spartans 'Go passer by, to tell the Lacedaemonians, that here we lie having obeyed their commands' (Herodotus 7.228.2).

The battles of Salamis and Plataea

The Greek defenders were now forced to face the reality that Xerxes had a clear route to march through central Greece and from there to Athens. The Athenians began a mass evacuation of their city, having come to the difficult decision that is was better to sacrifice the city in order to save the population, who were moved to the islands of Salamis and Aegina, as well as the city of Troizen in the eastern Peloponnese. The Greek fleet made its way to Salamis as well. Both the evacuation and the movement of the fleet were in response to an oracle the Athenians had received from Delphi at the start of the Persian invasion. The oracle stated:

> The rest will be taken, all lying within the boundary of Cecrops
> > And that of the hollow of sacred Cithaeron.
> > But a wall made of wood does farsighted Zeus to Tritogenes grant
> > Alone and unravaged, to help you and your children.
> > Do not await peacefully the horse and the foot,
> > The arm gigantic that comes from the mainland;
> > Withdraw, turn your backs, though someday you will meet face to face.
> > O Salamis Divine, the children of women you will yet destroy
> > While Demeter is scattered or while she is gathered (Herodotus 7.141.3–4)

Now, these oracles are often ambiguous, and an official response to a state sanctioned question such as this one elicited much debate as the Athenians attempted to decipher the exact meaning of the words – specifically, what the 'wooden walls' referred to. Some believed it was a reference to an old wooden palisade on the Acropolis, while the majority, led by Themistocles, felt they referred to the Athenian fleet, which meant they should use their ships to withdraw from Athens to the island of Salamis, from which they could be protected by the navy. The Persians invaded Attica and a deserted Athens in September 480; those few stubborn defenders who had remained in the city and entrenched themselves on the Acropolis were killed.

With Athens abandoned, the Athenians and the rest of the Hellenic League began discussing their next move. The Peloponnesian states maintained their stance of wanting to fortify the Isthmus and fall back behind the wall which they had already commenced building, particularly as they had received news that a portion of the Persian army was making for the Isthmus. The Greek fleet was still anchored at Salamis and their commanders were beginning to get a bit anxious, worried that the larger Persian fleet would corner them. The Athenians had contributed the greatest number of ships – 180 to be exact – and their commanders, headed by Themistocles, urged the fleet to stay put, but the size of their contribution did not give them any more authority, especially as control of the entire fleet technically fell to the Spartan general Eurybiades. News that Athens had fallen to the Persians created mass panic amongst the other naval contingents, all of whom thought the best course of action was to abandon Salamis and retreat to the Isthmus. Themistocles met with Eurybiades and the other commanders in an attempt to sway them, urging them to hold fast at Salamis rather than flee, but his pleas were rebuffed by his opponents who had set their minds firmly on flight.

In the meantime, the much-depleted Persian fleet had arrived and gathered east of Salamis. As the Greek commanders waffled about whether to hold their position or withdraw, the Persians fretted about whether or not the Greek fleet would try to slip away and avoid an engagement. Thus, both sides were undecided with regards to their course of action. According to Herodotus, the battle at Salamis came about entirely because of the wily machinations of Themistocles. Once he realized that he would not be able to sway the Greeks towards fight instead of flight, he tried a drastically different approach. The story goes that Themistocles sent his most trusted slave to the Persians with the following message for Xerxes:

> I have been sent here by the commander of the Athenians without the knowledge of the other Hellenes, for he happens to favour the cause of the King and wants your side to prevail over that of the Hellenes. I have come to tell you that the Hellenes are utterly terrified and are planning to flee, and that you now have the opportunity to perform the most glorious of all feats if you do not stand by and watch them escape, for they are in great disagreement with one another and will not stand up to you; indeed you will see them fighting a naval battle against themselves, those favouring your side opposing those who do not. (Herodotus 8.74.2–3)

The purpose of this visit was to persuade Xerxes that the Greek fleet was about to withdraw, and further, that he should attack immediately or risk looking his chance. Whether this story is factual us up for debate, but regardless, whether at Themistocles' urging to not, the Persian fleet began to manoeuvre into an offensive position under the cover of darkness. Their strategy was to drive the Greek fleet into open water, where their smaller size would put them at a distinct disadvantage. While all of this was going on through the night, the Greek commanders remained locked in debate, oblivious to Xerxes' actions. Upon receiving word of the Persian movement, however, they were forced to make a decision. The Athenians pressed their colleagues to attack instead of retreat, but the others continued to resist this idea. It was the desertion of a ship from the Persian side whose commander confirmed the news that the Greeks had essentially been surrounded by Xerxes' fleet that tipped the scales: the realization that any chance of flight had been cut off decided the matter. The decision to stay and fight was made. The Greeks boarded their ships and prepared for battle.

Things went poorly for the Persians from the start. The larger size of the Persian fleet proved a huge handicap in the confined space of the channel: the ships essentially became locked in a naval traffic jam, making it impossible to hold any semblance of a formation. The Greeks had anticipated this very scenario, and held back until the Persian fleet was very clearly in disarray, at which point they aggressively attacked. The Athenian and Aeginetian ships led the charge, ramming the floundering Persian vessels, causing even greater chaos as the damaged ships blocked the sound ships 'For since the Hellenes fought the naval battle in disciplined order and remained in their ranks, while the barbarians failed to hold their positions and made no moves that might have followed a sensible plan, the battle was bound to turn out as it did' (Herodotus 8.86.1). Now under constant pressure from the Greeks, the Persians attempted to turn and withdraw, creating even greater disorder. 'Most of their fleet was destroyed when the ships in the lead turned to flee, because those deployed behind them were trying to sail past so as to perform some spectacular feat before the King, and they collided with the leading ships from their own side who were in flight' (Herodotus 8.89.2). Some of the Persian ships even resorted to ramming vessels on their own side in an attempt to escape, most notably Artemisia, who found herself trapped between an Attic ship and a friendly ship belonging to the Calyndians. She made the decision to ram the Calyndian ship, which worked out to her advantage.

> For when the trierarch of the Attic ship saw that she was ramming a ship of the barbarians, he assumed that Artemisia's vessel was either a Greek ship or one that was deserting from the barbarians and now fighting for the Hellenes, so he turned away from her ship to attack others. (Herodotus 8.87.4)

Xerxes also observed Artemisia's actions, but he believed her to have sunk a Greek ship, to which he uttered the statement 'My men have become women, and my women, men!' (Herodotus 8.88.3). The Athenian ships continued to mow down the enemy ships that were trying to escape in increasing numbers. Those that did evade the Athenians were immediately ambushed by the Aeginetian contingent, which lay in wait for them in the strait between the site of the main battle and the open waters that led to the Bay of Phaleron. By the end of the day the Greek fleet had won a resounding victory: the Persians had lost over 200 ships before managing to retreat to the Bay of Phaleron.

The defeat at Salamis was a huge blow to Xerxes, primarily because he had lost such a significant portion of his fleet. Shortly after the battle he sent the remainder of the fleet back to Persian territory, while he himself marched home with a portion of the army. The remainder of his troops wintered in northern Greece under the command of Mardonius, the man who had been responsible for the initial Persian forays into Greece prior to Darius' expedition and who had urged Xerxes to invade Greece. One of the first things Mardonius did was to make overtures towards the Athenians in an attempt to persuade them to switch sides. He sent the Macedonian king Alexander I as envoy to Athenians on his behalf because 'he knew that the disaster that had befallen the Persians at sea had been accomplished mainly by the Athenians, he fully anticipated that if they were on his side, he would easily gain control over the sea, which was certainly a correct assumption' (Herodotus 8.136.2–3). Alexander informed the Athenians that he had been sent by Mardonius bearing a message from Xerxes. If the Athenians allied themselves with the Persian cause Xerxes would order Mardonius to 'give them back their land, and then let them have another land of their choice in addition, which they may govern independently. And if they wish to come to an agreement with me, you are to rebuild all the sanctuaries that I burned down' (Herodotus 8.140.2). The Spartans, when they caught word of this, were quick to send envoys to the Athenians, begging them not to leave the League. The envoys denounced Alexander as a tyrant supporting a tyrant, acting as a puppet for Mardonius. They urged the Athenians to hold fast, acknowledging that they had suffered greatly in the course of the war. As compensation for their losses the Lacedaemonians and their allies offered to 'support and maintain your women and all other members of your household who cannot serve in the military for as long as the war continues' (Herodotus 8.142.4). The Athenians remained loyal, rejecting Alexander's offers and reassuring the Spartans of their steadfastness, stating:

> It was quite natural for the Lacedaemonians to fear we would come to an agreement with the barbarian, but nevertheless, we think it disgraceful that you became so frightened, since you are well aware of the Athenians' disposition, namely, that there is no amount of gold anywhere on earth so great, nor any country that surpasses others so much in beauty and fertility, that we would accept it as a reward for medizing and enslaving Hellas. (Herodotus 8.144.1)

This encounter provided the Athenians with a valuable bargaining chip, which they used to wring out a promise from the Spartans that they would abandon their fortified position south of the Isthmus to come north and face the Persians. When Mardonius received word that his proposal had been rejected by the Athenians he immediately set out first through Thessaly, then Boeotia, before arriving in a still deserted Athens, as the Athenians were still at Salamis. Upon reaching Athens, Mardonius once again sent the Athenians a message offering to give them back their land if they would medize. Once again, the Athenians remained steadfast in their refusal to betray the Greek cause. Their ire with the Spartans and Peloponnesian allies, however, was increasing with each passing day. Although the risk of Athenian defection forced the Spartans into a corner, they continued to delay at home, postponing their decision to send an army north. The Athenians even went so far as to send envoys to Sparta to chastise them for their inactivity.

You, on the other hand, came to us utterly terrified that we would make an agreement with the Persian, but now, when you are well aware of our determination and have learned that we would never betray Hellas, and now just as the wall you are extending across the isthmus is nearing completion, we find that you pay no attention to the Athenians. You made an agreement with us to oppose the barbarian in Boeotia, but you have betrayed us and have allowed him to invade Attica. So you have provoked and enraged the Athenians by your improper conduct. But at this time they urge you to send out your army as quickly as possible to join ours...
(Herodotus 9.7.1–2)

The Spartans, realising that if the Athenians were ever to change their minds and join the Persians, the wall across the Isthmus would do little to protect them 'sent out 5,000 Spartans, with seven helots appointed to accompany each one, and assigned Pausanias son of Cleombrotus to lead them into battle' (Herodotus 9.10.1). These 5,000 Spartan hoplites were accompanied by thousands of other Peloponnesian hoplites and infantry, all marching north to face the Persians.

Upon receiving the news that this army was coming his way, Mardonius bade a hasty retreat from Athens having 'demolished all walls, buildings, and sanctuaries still standing, leaving everything in a heap of ruins, and then set Athens of fire and retreated before Pausanias and his troops arrived at the isthmus' (Herodotus 9.13.2). Mardonius made for the plains of Boeotia, as they would provide suitable terrain for cavalry, and cavalry remained the strongest arm of the Persian army. He made camp and settled down to await the arrival of the Greek force, which had gathered itself together at the Isthmus, received favourable omens from the sacrifices, and was now en route to Boeotia.

Upon arriving in Boeotia, the Greek army made the sensible choice to station themselves on the foothills of Mount Cithaeron in Erythrai, preferring to hold the high ground and avoid the cavalry-friendly plains below, where the Persians were camped along the Asopos River. Mardonius attempted to draw them out by using psychological tricks, he:

> ...sent against them his entire corps of cavalry under the command of Masistios...the horsemen rode out against the Hellenes and charged them by regiment, one and another, doing significant harm to them and insulting them as they did so by calling them 'women'. (Herodotus 9.20.3)

The Megarians faced the brunt of these attacks and finally reached a point where they could no longer withstand them. The Athenians volunteered to replace them, sending 300 men to assume their position at the forefront of the Greeks, along with the archers. The Persian cavalry continued to charge the infantry. In the course of the fighting, Masistios was killed. Upon realizing this, the Persian cavalry made a charge to try and retrieve his corpse, a scenario that could have ended in complete disaster for the Athenians who noticed that the cavalry was:

> ...no longer charging them in regiments, but was now in a mass formation, they shouted to the rest of the army for help. And as all the infantry rushed to assist them, a bitter struggle was fought over the corpse. Now, for as long as the 300 Athenians were there alone, they were in danger of being badly beaten; indeed, they were beginning to abandon the corpse when the main body of infantry came to their aid. Then it was the horsemen who could no longer stand their ground. Not only did they fail to retrieve the corpse, but they now lost other horsemen in addition to their commander. And so the drew back about 2 stades and discussed what they should do. In view of the fact that they had no leader, they decided to ride back to Mardonius. (Herodotus 9.23.1–2)

This victory against the formidable Persian cavalry did a great deal to boost morale in the Greek camp. So much so that they made the decision to abandon the high ground and descend into Plataea. They made camp near the Spring of Gargaphia, thereby ensuring regular access to a water source. The Greek army drew up its lines, deploying in national contingents. The Spartans and other Lacedaemonian hoplites took the right wing, supported by light-armed helot infantry, next to them were the

Tegeans, the center was held by the bulk of the Peloponnesian troops: Corinthians, Arcadians from Orchomenos, Sicyonians, Epidaurians, Troisenians, Lepreonians, a contingent from Mycenae and Tiryns, Phleiasians, Hermionians, and a group of Poteidaians from the Chalcidice in northern Greece. The Athenians took the left wing, with the Megarians and Plataeans posted alongside them, next to the Megarians were contingents from Eretria, Styra (both on the island of Euboea), Chalcidians, Ambraciots and Anactorians from the north-western part of Greece, troops from the islands of Cephallania and Leucas on the west coast, as well as men from the island of Aegina off the coast of Attica. The majority of these troops were hoplites. In response to the arrival of the Greeks at Plataea, Mardonius marched to meet them and drew up his forces. His army contained contingents from several Greek territories, including the Boeotians, Locrians, Malians, Thessalians, and some Phocians. As per tradition, prior to battle each side conducted sacrifices to see if the omens were favourable: both received the news that battle would go in their favour only if they fought to defend themselves, not if they initiated combat. The situation thus reached a stalemate, as neither Pausanias nor Mardonius was willing to risk ignoring the omens. The Persian cavalry continued to harass the Greeks, accompanied by the Thebans. The Greeks then received a night-time message informing them that Mardonius had become impatient with waiting and planned to attack the next day. Indeed, Mardonius sent a herald to taunt the Spartans in the hopes of goading them into battle. When the Spartans did not react to this by advancing forward, Mardonius once again sent out his cavalry who:

> ...rode out and attacked, inflicting injuries on the entire Greek army with their javelins and arrows, for they were mounted archers and it was impossible for the Hellenes to close with them. They also blocked and destroyed the Spring of Gargaphia, which had been the source of water for the whole Greek army (Herodotus 9.49.2)

The Greek army now found itself in dire straits without water and running low on supplies. The generals came to the conclusion that they had no choice but to retreat towards the city of Plataea if the Persians did not offer up battle before the end of the day. In the meantime, the cavalry continued cause a great deal of trouble, only withdrawing with nightfall. The Greeks immediately mobilized and began their retreat, encamping just outside the city. The following morning, Mardonius discovered the Greeks had departed and set off in pursuit, for he hoped to catch the Greek army while they were still in disarray rather than drawn up for battle. Unbeknownst to him, when he sent his Persian troops across the River Asopos he was not directing them against the entirety of the Greek army, but only against the Lacedaemonians and Tegeans, as the Athenians on the left wing were almost to the city walls, while the right wing was still retreating towards the city. When Pausanias perceived that the bulk of the Persian cavalry were making for his men, he sent a messenger to the Athenians requesting aid, or, if their hoplites were unable to leave their position, to at least send archers as back up. The Athenians immediately set out to help 'but along the way they were attacked by Greek allies of the King who were posted opposite them, and this attack caused them such distress that they were no longer able to go to their aid' (Herodotus 9.61.1). Left to face the bulk of Mardonius' army on their own, the Lacedaemonians and Tegeans engaged in a fierce battle. For a while, the Persians were able to hold the hoplites off with their archers, but when they finally advanced things began to turn in the Greeks favour, particularly when they came close enough to engage in close-combat fighting, for:

> The Persians were not inferior in courage or strength, but they did not have hoplite arms, and besides, they were untrained and no match for their opponents in tactical skill. They were dashing out beyond the front lines individually or in groups of 10, joining together in larger or smaller bands, and charging right into the Spartan ranks, where they perished. (Herodotus 9.62.3)

At the center of the Persian attack was Mardonius, who fought on horseback alongside the best of the Persians. The Persians resisted fiercely until Mardonius and his elite guard fell. Mardonius' death signalled panic amongst the remaining Persian troops who turned in flight towards their camp, giving way before the Spartans and their allies. Only the cavalry remained steadfast, fighting furiously to protect their retreating infantry. The Boeotian cavalry were particularly notable for their actions in defending their fleeing allies. In the meantime, the Athenians and the rest of the left wing managed to push through and join up with the Lacedaemonians and Tegeans, who had drawn up outside the Persian camp. They assaulted the defenses of the camp, which the Persians were tenaciously defending, until '… by their valour and perseverance, the Athenians mounted the wall and tore it down, and the Hellenes streamed in' (Herodotus 9.70.2). The Persians and their allies were now trapped within the confines of their camp and slaughtered by the victorious Greeks. Those who survived fled back to Asia Minor.

The Greek victory at Plataea removed the Persian threat. The allied states of the Hellenic League had done the impossible and driven Xerxes' army from mainland Greece, despite being vastly outnumbered. They now directed their attention against those states that had dared to medize, considering them betrayers of Greek freedom. The Thebans received particularly harsh treatment, as they had remained the staunchest defenders of the Persian army throughout their invasion of Greece. The Hellenic League held a meeting and concluded that Thebes needed to be punished. They first sent messengers demanding that the Thebans surrender their pro-Persian leaders. When the citizens refused to do so, the Greeks laid siege to the city. After 19 days of destruction the Theban leaders voluntarily gave themselves up in order to spare their city any additional hardship. Rather than allow them a trial, Pausanias sent these men to Corinth and had them executed.

CHAPTER 2

THE PELOPONNESIAN WAR

The precursor to war

THE PELOPONNESIAN WAR WAS A PIVOTAL period for the Greek world: militarily, socially, politically and economically. Our primary source is Thucydides, an Athenian citizen and general who fought in the war. His *Peloponnesian War* recounts the events of the period up to 411, when it abruptly ends. The latter years of the war are recounted by Xenophon, another Athenian, in his *Hellenica*. The origins of the war are tied into a complex and convoluted series of events: there was no one particular action that set it off. At the base of it all were the two major players: Athens and Sparta, both of whom had played pivotal roles in the Persian wars.

Following the Persian defeat at Plataea, the Spartans began a campaign to liberate the Greek cities of the Persian Empire. This ended abruptly, despite its success, when Pausanias the leader was recalled home on charges of inappropriate behaviour. Athens was quick to take Sparta's place, creating an alliance of states with the dual purpose of attacking Persia and preventing another Persian invasion of Greece. This alliance was formally established in 477 and came to be known as the Delian League, as its treasury was housed on the sacred island of Delos. The member states swore an oath to contribute funds/resources/manpower to the cause.

The terms of the oath were inscribed on a block of lead, which was dropped into the sea, with the idea being that the alliance would hold true and the states be bound to it until the lead rose to the surface again. All of the member states were meant to have equal rights and authority, however, the balance of power shifted rapidly to the Athenians. Nonetheless, the League did serve its purpose, achieving a series of victories against the Persians, most notable at the battle of the Eurymedon in 466, where the Athenian general Cimon achieved a stunning victory both on land and at sea, destroying a sizeable portion of the Persian fleet and effectively eliminating any lingering threat against Greece.

The League faced a major setback in 459 when they contributed 200 ships to aid the Egyptians in a revolt against Persian rule. This proved to be a disastrous decision when, after four years and some victories for Egypt and her allies, the Persians crushed the uprising. The Persian general Megabyzus:

> ...defeated the Egyptians and their allies in a battle, and drove the Hellenes out of Memphis, and at length shut them up in the island of Prosopitis, where he besieged them for a year and six months. At last, draining the canal of its waters, which he diverted into another channel, he left their ships high and dry and joined most of the island to the mainland, and then marched over on foot and captured it. (Thucydides 1.109.4)

The loss of these ships drastically weakened the effectiveness of the Delian League and it gave the Athenians an excuse to move the treasury from Delos to Athens, as they felt that the island could no longer be safeguarded. This effectively gave the Athenians sole control over the treasury. Despite the loss in Egypt, the League continued to campaign against Persia until 449, when Persia and the Athenians negotiated the Peace of Callias. Many of the smaller states felt that with creation of this treaty, the League had become obsolete, and they wanted out. Athens, however, did not see things quite the same way and

Fragment of an inscription. This is part of a tribute list recording payment to Athens from Paros, Naxos, Andros, Melos, Siphnos, Eretria, and Thera. (Metropolitan Museum of Art Open Content Program)

outright refused to allow it. At this point we can safely say that the Delian League had become the Athenian Empire.

The Spartans had not joined the Delian League, but created an alliance of their own, known as the Peloponnesian League. The name is a bit of a misnomer, as not all of its members came from the Peloponnese, several were Boeotian cities from north of Attica. Unlike the Delian League, the Peloponnesian League worked on an *ad hoc* basis: it only went into action when one of its member states faced a security threat. Thus, it was more a defensive alliance, as opposed to the Delian League, which acted

Red Figure column crater. Hoplite arming himself for battle. Citizen soldiers like this one played a significant role in the Peloponnesian War. (Metropolitan Museum of Art Open Content Program)

very much on the offensive. Thucydides sums up the differences in policy between the Spartans and the Athenians when he writes:

> The policy of Sparta was not to exact tribute from her allies, but merely to secure their subservience to her interests by establishing oligarchies among them; Athens, on the contrary, had by degrees deprived hers of their ships, and imposed instead contributions in money on all except Chios and Lesbos. Both found their resources for this war separately to exceed the sum of their strength when the alliance flourished intact. (Thucydides 1.19.1)

If Athens was preoccupying itself with Persia and the Delian League, while Sparta had effectively withdrawn to its territory in the Peloponnese, how on earth did war, especially on a scale hitherto unknown break out? Well, it all started with a natural disaster. In 464 a sizeable earthquake wreaked havoc in Sparta. Not surprisingly, some of the Messenians in Ithome used the ensuing chaos as an opportunity to revolt against their Spartan overlords. Sparta sent out a request for help to a number of states, including Athens. The Athenian statesman, Cimon, persuaded his fellow citizens to send a small force to their aid. If we believe Thucydides it seems the Spartans were particularly keen to get the Athenians involved because of 'their reputed skill in siege operations; a long siege had taught the Spartans their own deficiency in this art...' (Thucydides 1.102.2). Upon the arrival of Cimon and his troops the Spartans appear to have changed their minds and chosen to reject the Athenian assistance, dismissing them in short order. Needless to say, this did not go over well in Athens, as the Athenians were 'conscious of having done nothing to merit such treatment from the Spartans; and the instant they returned home they broke off the alliance which had been made...' (Thucydides 1.102.4). This Athenian rejection marks a 14-year period (460–446), sometimes called the First Peloponnesian War, of ever increasing tension between the Spartans and the Athenians. Both states sought to ally themselves with the enemies of their opponent, creating political upheaval and military conflicts. The Athenians immediately allied themselves with the city of Argos, a long-standing rival of Sparta, as well as Thessaly. The Thessalian alliance was a strategic move to acquire cavalry and horses. The Spartans were still dealing with the rebellion in Ithome and in 457/6 the rebels finally surrendered themselves under the conditions that they would be allowed to leave the Peloponnese. This request was granted. The majority of the refugees looked to the Athenians for assistance and were settled at Naupactus, a decision that would work to the benefit of the Athenians in the coming years. Around this time the Athenians also began the construction of the Long Walls, which would connect the city with their harbour at the Piraeus. The re-fortification of the Athens had begun at the instigation of Themistocles in 478. The decision to build these walls would prove to be an insightful one.

The outbreak of war

The first notable battle took place in 457 at Tanagra in Boeotia. The Spartans were heavily outnumbered, but nonetheless prevailed, partially due to the fact that the Thessalian cavalry switched sides mid-battle; however, both armies experienced heavy losses. The Spartans used this as an opportunity to make an incursion into Athenian territory by invading the lands of the Megarians (Athenian allies) and cutting down the fruit trees. This move was a precursor to what would become standard Spartan policy: ravaging Athenian land and destroying their crops. The Athenians were not daunted by their defeat at Tanagra nor the attack on the Megarid. As soon as the Spartans had returned home, the Athenians soundly defeated a Boeotian force, with the result that a large portion of Central Greece fell under Athenian control. Following this victory, Athens went on the offensive. In 456 they sent a fleet of 50 ships to raid and ravage the Laconian coast, burning the Spartan shipyard at their main port of Gytheon. They also took control of the city of Chalcis, located at the entrance of the Gulf of Corinth. The possession of Chalcis along with Naupactus, which the Athenians had already settled with the Messenian refugees from Ithome, gave Athens a secure naval foothold in the region. This naval expedition was not only strategically important for the Athenians, it also served to highlight the weakness of the Spartan navy, an issue they would struggle with repeatedly in the early and middle stages of the war.

Despite these successes the Athenians were struggling with setbacks. This was largely due to stretching their resources by trying to fight on two fronts: they were engaging Sparta and her allies at home, while also still dealing with Persian affairs. As we have already seen, the loss of a large portion of their fleet in Egypt after the failed uprising hit them hard. On top of all this, several members of the Delian League were making noise about wanting to pull out of the alliance. As a result, Athens was trying to contend with a number of military and political issues simultaneously. On the other hand, the Spartans lacked the imperialistic ambitions of the Athenians. Although they were prepared to fulfil their obligations to the other members of the Peloponnesian League, they had no desire to venture out of the Peloponnese on their own accord. All of these factors led to the creation in 451 of a five-year peace treaty between Athens and Sparta, as well as the Thirty Years' Peace between Sparta and Argos, tempering their alliance with Athens. Things remained relatively quiet for a few years, but in 447/6 the Boeotians made a concerted effort to throw off the Athenian yoke and regain their independence. In the ensuing conflict, the Boeotians managed to capture a large number of Athenian hostages, whom they were then able to use as a bargaining chip to force Athens to withdraw from Boeotia, relinquishing all of their conquered territory in the region with the exception of Plataea. The success of the Boeotian revolt instigated uprisings in several other Athenian-controlled states, notably the Euboeans and the Megarians. The Megarians went so far as to request and receive the assistance of a Spartan force, led by the king Pleistonax, who 'marched into Attica as far as Eleusis and Thria, ravaging the country...' (Thucydides 1.114.2). Upon receiving news of this, the Athenian general and statesman Pericles marched his army in haste from Euboea to confront the Spartans, who withdrew without engaging in battle as soon as Pericles arrived. Pericles then marched straight back to Euboea, to finish putting down the uprising there. The First Peloponnesian War came to an end later in 446 when Athens and Sparta agreed to terms for a 30-year peace. Both sides were allowed to maintain their alliances and keep conquered territory, but it did nothing to ease the tension between the two states and a deep mutual suspicion remained firm in place. In 441 the island of Samos rose up against Athens: the Spartans were keen to help, as it would provide an excuse to go to war with Athens, but they were outvoted by the other members of the Peloponnesian League, who preferred to maintain the tenuous peace. Despite this, by 440 it was becoming quite evident that a full-on war between Athens and Sparta was inevitable.

As tensions between Athens, Sparta, and their respective allies simmered, Sparta was receiving increasing pressure to act against the imperialistic tendencies of the Athenians, particularly from the Corinthians. In 435 the Corinthians became embroiled in a dispute between two of their colonies: Corcyra and Epidamnus. The Corinthians chose to side with the Epidamnians and began amassing a sizeable fleet with which they could quash the Corcyrians as:

Pericles is one of the most important figures in Athenian history. A celebrated military man and statesman, he was responsible for guiding Athens through the first decade of the Peloponnesian War. His popularity was such that he held the elected position of *strategos* (general) for several consecutive years. His approach to the war was considered controversial, as he refused to meet the Spartans on the field; preferring to fall back behind the city walls and instead harass them with hit and run tactics, however it did lead Athens from success to success. Pericles also began a massive civic building program in the 440s and 430s, most notably rebuilding the temples on the Acropolis that had been destroyed by the Persians. He died of the plague in 429.

> ...exasperated by the war with the Corcyrians, they spent the whole of the year after the engagement and that succeeding it in building ships, and in straining every nerve to form an efficient fleet; rowers being drawn from the Peloponnese and the rest of Hellas by the inducement of large bounties. (Thucydides 1.31.1)

In retaliation, the Corcyrians had formed an alliance with the Athenians, arguing that an alliance between Athens and Corcyra would not breach the conditions of the 30 years peace between Sparta and Athens. Their reasoning was that they were a neutral state, a member of neither the Peloponnesian League nor the Delian League. Further, they argued that 'one of the express provisions of the treaty is that it shall be open to any Hellenic state that is neutral to join whichever side it pleases' (Thucydides 1.35.2). The Athenians agreed to support Corcyra and entered into an alliance with them, sending 10 triremes to support their cause. Although the Corinthians won the ensuing naval battle, they nonetheless argued that Athens had no right to become involved in this affair. When the Athenians sent an additional 20 ships as reinforcements, the Corinthians spoke out against them, stating, 'You do wrong, Athenians, to begin war and break the treaty. Engaged in chastising our enemies, we find you placing yourselves in our path in arms against us' (Thucydides 1.53.2), to which the Athenians replied:

> Neither are we beginning war, Peloponnesians, nor are we breaking the treaty; but these Corcyrians are our allies, and we are come to help them. So if you want to sail anywhere else, we place no obstacle in your way; but if you are going to sail against Corcyra, or any of her possessions, we shall do our best to stop you. (Thucydides 1.53.2)

The Corinthians' underlying fear was that an alliance between the two states would make Athens invincible at sea, and so they pleaded their case to the League in an attempt to curb further Athenian expansion.

In addition to this, the Corinthians had a second bone to pick with the Athenians. The city of Potidaea (founded by the Corinthians), located in the Chalcidice on the border of Macedonia, was a member of the Delian League; however, in 433 at the urging of the Macedonian king Perdiccas, who was technically an ally of Athenians and so breaking his own agreement with them, they revolted along with several other cities, against the Athenians to form a Chalcidician League. Not surprisingly, there were repercussions. The initial Athenian response to Perdiccas' perfidy and plans was to do the following: the Athenians '...were just then sending off 30 ships and 1,000 hoplites to Perdiccas' territory...they instructed those in command of the ships to take hostages of the Potidaeans, to raze the wall, and to be on their guard against the revolt of the neighbouring cities' (Thucydides 1.57.5). Realising they had angered the Athenians the Potidaeans sent envoys to the Peloponnese and obtained a promise that if Athens attacked Potidaea, the Spartans would invade Attica. Having received this surety, the Potidaeans felt things were going in their favour and they 'at last entered into league with the Chalcidians and Bottiaeans, and revolted' (Thucydides 1. 58.1). Potidaea and the Chalcidice provided a substantial source of tribute for the Athenian Empire; the loss of this revenue would be a huge blow. And so the Athenians made the decision to march on Potidaea. They sent 2,000 Athenian hoplites and a fleet of 40 ships north against the Potidaeans and other cities in revolt. These troops joined up with the advance force of 1,000 hoplites and 30 ships, which had earlier been sent out. They took the cities of Therme and Pydna, forced a new alliance with Perdiccas, and in 432 set out for Potidaea. The Spartans had not fulfilled their promise of invading Attica, but the Corinthians and other Peloponnesians had indeed sent a relief force to the aid of the Potidaeans. In the initial battle outside the city walls, the Athenians were by and large victorious, and the defenders fled to take refuge behind the walls. The Athenians lay siege to the city, bolstered by the arrival of an additional 1,600 hoplites. With Potidaea encircled, the Athenians also sent out a force to ravage both the Chalcidice and Bottica.

As far as the Corinthians were concerned, the Athenian attack on Potidaea was a clear act of war that made the 30-year truce of 446 null and void. In 432 the Corinthians presented a case for war at a meeting of the Peloponnesian League. They chastised the Spartans for not acting against Athens.

> Time after time was our voice raised to warn you of the blows about to be dealt to us by the Athenians, and time after time, instead of taking the trouble to ascertain the worth of our warnings, you contented yourselves with suspecting the speakers of being inspired by private interest. And so, instead of calling these allies together before the blow fell, you have delayed and do so till we are smarting under it; and of the allies it is not unfitting that we make this speech for we have very great complaints of high handed treatment by the Athenians and of neglect by you. (Thucydides 1.68.2)

However, the Corinthians were not the only envoys to pitch their case to the Spartans; Athens also happened to have some representatives in town when the assembly had gathered, and they asked for permission to defend themselves and their actions against the case put forward by the Corinthians. The speech Thucydides provides us with is an unabashed defence of Athenian foreign policy, particularly in the wake of Xerxes' invasion:

> Surely, Spartans, neither by the patriotism that we displayed at that crisis, nor by the wisdom of our counsels, do we merit our extreme unpopularity with the Hellenes, nor least unpopularity for our empire. That empire we acquired not by violence, but because you were unwilling to prosecute to its conclusion the war against the barbarian, and because the allies attached themselves to us and spontaneously asked us to assume the command. And the nature of the case first compelled us to advance our empire to its present height; fear being our principal motive, though honour and interest afterwards came in. And at last, when almost all hated us, when some had already revolted and had been subdued, when

you had ceased to be the friends that you once were, and had become objects of suspicion and dislike, it appeared no longer sage to give up our empire; especially as all who left us would fall to you. And no one can quarrel with a people for making, in matters of tremendous risk, the best provision that it can for its interest. (Thucydides 1.75.1–5)

The Spartans listened to both cases and deliberated over what the best course of action should be. This was not because they thought Athens might be in the right, but rather, on account of the fact that Athens would be immensely difficult to defeat. The Spartan king, Archidamus, astutely warned his compatriots that:

Confidence might possibly be felt in our superiority in hoplites and population, which will enable us to invade and devastate their lands. But the Athenians have plenty of other land in their empire, and can import what they want by sea. Again, if we are to attempt an insurrection of their allies, these will have to be supported with a fleet, most of them being islanders. What then is to be our war? For unless we can either beat them at sea, of deprive them of the revenues which feed their navy, we shall met with little but disaster. Meanwhile our honour will be pledged to keeping on, particularly if it be the opinion that we began the quarrel. (Thucydides 1.81.1–5)

Archidamus' words would prove prophetic over the coming years; however, at the time they were disregarded. Sparta put the matter to a vote and the majority found Athens guilty of breaking the treaty. According to Thucydides, Sparta did not vote for war solely on the argument that Athens had broken the peace or because of the arguments presented by their allies, but rather, that the overriding cause was a fear that Athenian power would continue to grow. With their decision made the Spartans did not immediately launch themselves into war. They sent Athens a series of injunctions, which included an order that Athens end the siege of Potidaea.

It was not only Corinth that had a serious issue with Athenian actions; Megara was expressing some major concerns as well.

Bust of a Greek general. The course of the Peloponnesian War was driven by the generals and politicians within each city state. (Metropolitan Museum of Art Open Content Program)

Following the Megarian revolt in 446, the Athenians instituted the Megarian Decree, which essentially banned the Megarians from using the marketplaces of all territory under Athenian control, an act which would severely hinder the ability of Megara to trade with other states. The intent of the Decree was to pressure the Megarians into breaking its alliance with Sparta, as the Athenians were concerned that the Spartans would use Megara as an access point from which they could invade Attica. Thus, a second injunction 'made it very clear to the Athenians that war might be prevented if they revoked the Megara decree…' (Thucydides 1.139.1). Finally, the island of Aegina, off the coast of Attica, had also rebelled in an attempt to throw off Athenian control. The island had been part of the Delian League since 458, but they felt that Athens was imposing far too much control over the island and its affairs. Much the same as with Megara, the rebellious attitude of Aegina was a substantial security threat for Athens, as the island could easily be used as a convenient naval base for Athens' enemies. As a final injunction, the Spartans demanded the Athenians respect the independence of Aegina. Athens refused to acknowledge or accept any of these injunctions. Still keen to avoid war, the Spartans sent an embassy to Athens bearing this ultimatum 'Sparta wishes the peace to continue, and there is no reason why it should not, if you would let the Hellenes be independent' (Thucydides 1.139.3). The Athenians convened an assembly to discuss this ultimatum. Pericles came forward and spoke virulently against accepting Sparta's demands. Where Archidamus had urged caution Pericles pushed for action, stating that Athens had innumerable resources at its disposal and that war would be in their favour, particularly emphasizing the advantages of Athenian sea power. He stated that although the Spartans may fortify cities and attack Athenian land:

> …it can never prevent our sailing into their country and raising fortifications there, and making reprisals with our powerful fleet. For our naval skill is of more use to us for service on land, than their military skill for service at sea. Familiarity with the sea they will not find an easy acquisition… (Thucydides 1.142.4–6).

The ultimatum was soundly rejected, peace negotiations broke down, and war became inevitable. From the very beginning there were hints that this war would be unlike anything that had come before, breaking the customs and norms of traditional Greek warfare in terms of tactics, rules, strategy and violence.

The Archidamian war

The first action of the war against the Athenians came not from Sparta, but from Boeotia, particularly Thebes. The Boeotians harboured no kind feelings towards the Athenians. Under the terms of the Thirty Years Peace, Athens had been forced to give up all of its conquered Boeotian territory, with the exception of Plataea. The fact that Athens had retained any foothold in Boeotia at all irked the Boeotian League, and so the Thebans marched on Plataea with a force of 300 hoplites and demanded the Plataeans turn their backs on the Athenians by joining the Boeotian League. The Plataeans refused to do so, in large part because Thebes and Plataea had a long-standing enmity. The Thebans caught the Plataeans off guard and managed to enter the city. While in the midst of negotiating terms, the Plataeans realized that there was only a scant Theban force on site. Feeling they could easily overpower the invaders the Plataeans began:

> Digging through the common walls of the houses, they thus managed to join each other without being seen going through the streets, in which they placed wagons without the beasts in them, to serve as a barricade, and arranged everything else as seemed suitable for the occasion. When everything had been done that circumstances permitted, they watched their opportunity and went out of their houses against the enemy. It was still night, though daybreak was at hand: in daylight their attack would be met by men full of courage and on equal terms with their assailants, while in darkness it would fall upon panic-stricken troops, who would also be at a disadvantage from their enemy's knowledge of the locality.

So they made their assault at once, and came to close quarters as
quickly as they could. (Thucydides.2.3.3–4).

The Thebans made a valiant attempt to rally and defend
themselves, but were forced into flight: disoriented, slipping in
mud after a rainy night, and unable to see where they were going
because of the quarter moon. The gates were shut against them,
effectively trapping them within the city walls. The largest group
of Thebans found themselves trapped in an empty building near
one of the city gates. Realising the futility of their situation, the
Thebans agreed to an unconditional surrender. In the meantime,
reinforcements from Thebes had arrived. They were too late to
prevent the night-time attack. As the events within the city had
all been rather unexpected, there were still a large number of
Plataean citizens outside the city walls, working the fields etc.
Thus, the Theban relief force hatched the plan of taking a number
of these individuals hostage, in the hopes that they would be
able to exchange them for the Thebans trapped inside the walls.
The Plataeans once again outwitted the Thebans, assuming
that they would take this course of action. They sent a herald
to the Thebans '…reproaching them for their unscrupulous
attempt to seize their city in time of peace, and warning them
against any outrage on those outside. Should the warnings be
disregarded, they threatened to put to death the men they had in
their hands, but added that, on the Thebans retiring from their
territory, they would surrender the prisoners to their friends'
(Thucydides.2.5.5). The Thebans agreed to these terms and
withdrew from Plataean territory. The Plataeans immediately
gathered their citizens inside the walls; having brought them to
safety, then executed the 180 Theban hostages. The events at
Plataea brought a clear and undeniable end to the thirty years
peace. Greece was now without a doubt divided and at war, and
Sparta adopted the mantle of liberators of Hellas.

These were the allies of Sparta: all the Peloponnesians within
the Isthmus except the Argives and Achaeans, who were neutral;

Pellene being the only Achaean city that first joined in the war... Outside the Peloponnesus the Megarians, Locrians, Boeotians, Phocians, Abraciots, Leucadians, and Anactorians. Of these, ships were furnished by the Corinthians, Megarians, Sicyonians, Pellenians, and Locrians. The other states sent infantry....That of Athens comprised of the Chians, Lesbians, Plataeans, the Messenians in Naupactus, most of the Arcanians, the Corcyraeans, Zacynthians, and some tributary cities in the following countries, namely, the seaboard part of Caria with its Dorian neighbours, Ionia, the Hellespont, the Thracian cities, the islands lying between the Peloponnese and Crete toward the east, and all the Cyclades except Melos and Thera. Of these, ships were furnished by Chios, Lesbos, and Corcyra, infantry and money by the rest. (Thucydides 2.9.2–5).

The first ten years of the war proper are referred to as the Archidamian War. From the outset both Sparta and Athens had a clear military strategy. The Athenians recognized the military superiority of the Spartan hoplites in pitched battled, and so they were determined to avoid engaging in set combat. Instead they followed the advice of Pericles and withdrew from the Attic countryside and retreated behind the city walls, abandoning their outlying territory. This made them reliant on their ships for supplies and other resources: so long as Athens maintained her naval superiority, these goods could be brought to the port at the Piraeus from allied territory and trade. From the Piraeus, supplies were transported to the city proper behind the safety of the Long Walls. The Athenians were banking on the idea that Sparta would eventually tire of waiting Athens out and enter peace negotiations via a stalemate, which would theoretically give Athens the upper hand. Nor were the Athenians just twiddling their thumbs behind the walls: they could still use their fleet to harass coastal territory belonging to their opponents, just at they had during the First Peloponnesian War. The Spartans, on the other hand, had a strategy based heavily on invading and ransacking Attic farmland and towns, with the thought that watching the destruction of their property would infuriate and frustrate the Athenians enough to force them out from behind their walls onto the battlefield in a traditional pitched battle. Or, if they still refused to do this, it would at least force them to come to terms. It is clear that at the start of the war, both sides were desirous of avoiding major bloodshed and battle; both hoped to achieve terms through a stalemate of sorts. Needless to say, the result was the complete opposite of these aims.

In 431 the Spartan forces and their allies invaded and laid waste to the countryside of Attica; but the Athenians did not sit by idly. They regularly used small parties of cavalry and light infantry to harass and impede the raiding parties. They also sent out a fleet of 100 ships carrying 1,000 hoplites and 400 archers. These were joined by a sizeable number of allied vessels. This fleet set sail for the Peloponnese with the intent of wreaking havoc on the coastal regions and taking control of as many cities as they could. Although the destruction of their crops was incredibly frustrating for the farmers and the loss of their land a raw wound for all the citizens, it did not manage to starve out the Athenians as it would in a typical siege. Thanks to the Long Walls connecting the city with the Piraeus, Athens managed to maintain access to supplies. Thus far, the Athenian strategy seemed to be working. Their populace was safe, if restless, behind the city walls, supplies were arriving from the harbour, their fleet had unimpeded control of the sea, and there was little the Spartans and their allies could do in retaliation. All of this changed in 430 when those same supply ships and walls brought plague to the city. The outbreak of plague in Athens had a devastating affect on the population, even their general, the man who had thus far directed the Athenian course of war – Pericles – fell victim to it. However, it did not break Athenian resolve. If anything, it spurred them on as they began to take increasingly more aggressive naval action against their opponents.

In 430/29 the Potidaeans were finally forced to recognize that they could no longer hold out against their besiegers. They made terms with the Athenians that would allow 'free passage for themselves, their children, wives and auxiliaries, with one garment apiece, the women with two, and a fixed sum of money for their journey' (Thucydides 2.70.3). Potidaea was then colonized by Athens and re-settled with peoples of their choosing. In the summer of 429, the Peloponnesians chose not to invade Attica, but instead focused on Plataea. Archidamus first tried to win them over through diplomacy, but the Plataeans refused to renounce their alliance with Athens. His offer rejected, Archidamus began an assault on the city walls. Fortunately for the Plataeans, the Spartans were not the most skilled at this, and they were able to counter every Peloponnesian attempt to compromise or breach the walls. Having failed to take the city by means of siege engines, palisades, and earthen mounds, the Peloponnesians began plans to besiege the city. Their first attempt was to burn the city, which would be quick and inexpensive, and although they managed to create 'a fire greater than anyone had ever yet seen produced by human agency…' (Thucydides 2.77.4), their plans had not taken into consideration the possible intervention of nature: a combination of wind and rain diverted and quenched the fire, saving the city from destruction. At this point the Peloponnesians only option was to begin a siege. They '…built a wall of circumvallation round the city, dividing the ground among the various cities present; a ditch being made within and without the lines, from which they got their bricks' (Thucydides 2.78.1). The Plataeans '…sent off their wives and children and oldest men and the mass of the non-combatants to Athens; so that the number of the besieged left in the place comprised 400 of their own citizens, 80 Athenians, and 110 women to bake their bread' (Thucydides 2.78.3). The siege lasted for over a year. The Athenians were fully engaged elsewhere, and the Plataeans had little hope of rescue. With their provisions running low and no way of replenishing them, the Plataean made a plan to escape by forcing their way out over walls the enemy had built around the city. Only about half of the defenders agreed to this plan, the others felt it was far too risky. Preparations were made, at which pointed the waited for the right moment to make their move, which took place on '...a stormy night of wind and rain without any moon...' (Thucydides 3.22.1). They chose their moment well and 212 Plataeans managed to break out and escape to Athens. Those who had remained in the city found themselves in dire straits. The Spartans made an attack on the walls that the Plataeans were unable to repel, given the small number of defenders remaining and the fact that they were on the brink of starvation. A herald was sent asking the Plataeans if they wished to voluntarily surrender their city and face trial at the hands of the Spartans. They agreed to these terms and relinquished themselves and their city. The Plataeans pleaded their case before the judges and asked that the city not be handed over to the Thebans for certain destruction. There was, of course, a detachment of Thebans present, and they spoke in retaliation against the Plataeans, fearing the Spartans might be lenient towards them. The Plataeans used the argument that the Thebans were not to be trusted as they had medized and sided with Xerxes during his invasion of Greece, betraying the homeland to a barbarian; while the Thebans countered by stating they had not done so willingly, however, the Plataeans had agreed to join the Athenians without any constraints. In the end, the Spartan judges determined that the Plataeans were a threat to their security and the Peloponnesian cause as they had rejected previous overtures from Sparta and her allies and defiantly refused to break from Athens. The concluded that they had:

> ...suffered evil at the hands of the Plataeans, they brought them in again one by one and asked each of them the same question, that is to say, whether they had done the Spartans and allies any service in the war; and upon their saying that they had not, took them out and slew them all without exception. The number of Plataeans thus massacred was not less than 200, with 25 Athenians who had shared in the siege. The women were taken as slaves. (Thucydides.3.68.1–2).

While the Peloponnesians were engaged at Plataea, the Athenians were dealing with a troubling uprising. In 428, the city of Mytilene on the island of Lesbos led a revolt against the Athenians. Mytilene had been one of the founding members of the Delian League, and the loss of the tribute and resources provided by the island would be a huge blow for the Athenians. Mytilene and most of the other Lesbian cities were of the opinion that the plague had weakened Athens both morally and physically, leading them to believe that there would be no immediate or effective response to a revolt and were thus uniting the island under Mytilenean control. The Athenians were alarmed at the possibility of losing Lesbos and took action. They sent a small fleet of 40 ships to the island, hoping to catch them unaware during a festival, however, the Mytileneans received notice of the fleets approach and prepared themselves as best they could. Several Mytilenean ships were sent out in an attempt to confront the Athenian vessels, but they were easily pushed back. A parley was then held and an armistice concluded, with the Mytileneans bound and determined to get the Athenian fleet to withdraw, which they eventually agreed to do. In the course of these peace talks, they also secretly sent envoys to Sparta and the Peloponnesian League to secure assistance in the event of a serious Athenian attack on the city. Mytilene and several other cities then renewed hostilities, making an attack on the Athenian camp. This was only a minor success and with nightfall they quickly withdrew behind their walls, where they chose to wait for reinforcements. More envoys were sent to Sparta seeking assurance of aid, and those who had been sent earlier spoke before the Spartans and their allies at Olympia. They argued that their rebellion was not dishonourable, and that they had only broken faith with the Athenians when they began to deny their allies independence. They pleaded with Sparta to accept them as allies and seize an opportunity to weaken Athens and seize the advantage.

The Spartans agreed to the proposal and accepted Lesbos as an ally. They commenced plans to invade Attica. In response to these events the Athenians dispatched an additional 100 ships to Lesbos. This caught the Spartans by surprise, as they seem to have believed the envoys when they said that the Athenians were short of spare ships, and so they withdrew to the Peloponnese, from where they made plans to send a small relief fleet to Lesbos, but this arrived too late. The Mytileneans were starving: the Athenians had blockaded the harbour, preventing resources from reaching the island. Meanwhile, within the city grain stores were low, and the oligarchic regime that controlled the city refused to distribute food to the frustrated and starving population, who in turn surrendered the city unconditionally to the Athenians; their only request was that they would be able to send envoys to Athens to defend the actions of the city. Having taken the city, the Athenians found themselves in a bit of a quandary, as they were divided on which punishment to mete out. They wanted to make an example of Mytilene so that other allied states would be hesitant to rebel, but they were not entirely sure as to how harsh they should be in their response. Opinions in Athens were divided but '…in the fury of the moment they determined to put to death not only the prisoners at Athens, but the whole adult male population of Mytilene, and to make slaves of the women and children' (Thucydides 3.36.2), thereby making a brutal statement about the risks of attempting to throw off the Athenian yoke. A ship was immediately sent to Mytilene bearing these terrible orders. However, the next day the Athenians began to regret the extreme harshness of their choices, especially as the majority of the population had actually been the ones to surrender the city to Athenians, feeling their own government had betrayed them. This realization led to a change of heart, and the decree was altered so that only those responsible for the revolt would be punished. A second ship was dispatched in great haste, with the crew rowing in shifts in an attempt to overtake the first ship. This second ship arrived just in time. The ringleaders were executed, while the city was stripped of its fleet and much of its territory.

Within the first few years of the war two things were becoming very clear: first, that this would not be a short or decisive engagement, but rather a long and drawn out event, and that the Spartans were at a distinct disadvantage when it came to naval warfare. The Athenians were the undisputed masters of the sea, and there was no way the outcome of this war would be determined entirely on land. The Spartans began the process of building and equipping a fleet. In 429, this fleet sailed out to challenge the Athenian fleet stationed at Naupactus. Naupactus was a strategically significant location, as it placed the Athenian fleet in a position from which they could send out naval sorties against enemy ships sailing from Corinth, the northern Peloponnese, and Boeotia. The Spartans may have built a fleet, but their inexperience in handling it was immediately apparent. Despite being outnumbered 47–20, the seasoned Athenian fleet routed the Spartans, sinking several of their ships and capturing 12. Soon afterwards, a fleet of 77 Peloponnesian ships made another attempt to wrest Naupactus from the Athenians. Although they had some initial success by pinning the Athenian fleet against the shoreline, hindering their speed and agility, their inexperience once again became apparent when the Athenian ships made a strategic retreat back to Naupactus, with all but one ship making it to the harbour where they drew up in preparation to defend themselves should the Peloponnesian ships attack.

> After a while the Peloponnesian ships came up, chanting the *paean* for their victory as they sailed on; the single Athenian ship remaining being chased by a Leucadian far ahead of the rest. But there happened to be a merchantman lying at anchor in the roadstead, which the Athenian ship found time to sail round, and struck the Leucadian in chase amidships and sank her. An exploit so sudden and unexpected produced a panic among the Peloponnesians; and having fallen out of order in the excitement of victory, some of them dropped their oars and stopped their way in order to let the main body come up…while others ran aground in the shallows, in their ignorance of the localities. (Thucydides 2.91.2–4).

The strung out line of Peloponnesian ships made easy targets for the Athenians who could not believe their luck at this reversal of fortunes. The Athenian ships sallied out and rammed the enemy vessels creating even greater chaos amongst the Peloponnesian fleet. In the end the Athenians managed to recapture most of the ships they had lost at the start of the engagement, as well as six Peloponnesian vessels. From this point on the Peloponnesians were, not surprisingly, reluctant to engage in any sort of naval conflict with the Athenians.

Sphacteria

Thus far, aside from the loss of Plataea and the outbreak of plague, things seemed to be going strongly in favour of the Athenians. This was largely due to their naval superiority and resistance to meeting the Spartans in pitched battle. In 425, things were progressing in their usual fashion. The Spartans once again led a Peloponnesian force into Attica, under the command of king Agis, to ravage the countryside in an attempt to force the Athenians out and into battle. At the same time, the Athenians sent a fleet of 40 ships to Sicily, stopping en route to assist the Corcyrians who were having some issues of their own. On board one of the ships was the general-elect, Demosthenes, who had a plan. Although the two generals in command of the fleet were eager to get to Corcyra and thence to Sicily, Demosthenes first ordered them to put in at Pylos on the south western corner of the Peloponnese. He wanted to turn this coastal town into a fortified post, from which the Athenians could send raids into Peloponnesian territory, ideally led by Messenian exiles who would push into Messenia proper and persuade the locals to rise up against Sparta. Demosthenes and his men settled down to the process of fortifying Pylos, keeping five ships as the bulk of the fleet sailed on. At first the Spartans at home in Lacedaemonia gave scant attention to this action, but when they realized that the Athenians had indeed fortified the area and did not appear to be leaving Agis and his troops in Attica reacted with much alarm and hastened south to Sparta.

When he heard the news that the Peloponnesians had mobilized, Demosthenes sent word to the Athenian fleet, which aborted its mission to Corcyra/Sicily and turned back to Pylos. Upon its arrival the Peloponnesian fleet was reluctant to engage the Athenian fleet directly, instead they chose to block off the entrances of the harbour to prevent the Athenians from entering and anchoring inside, a plan aided by the small island of Sphacteria which 'stretches along in a line close in front of the harbour and at once makes it safe and narrows its entrances, leaving a passage for 2 ships on the side nearest Pylos and the Athenian fortifications, and for 8 or 9 ships on that next to the mainland on the other side...' (Thucydides 4.8.6). They also landed a small force of hoplites on the island, in case the Athenians should decide to make use of it for themselves. While this idea seemed sensible, it would prove to be a disastrous decision. The Spartans launched an attack by land and sea on the Athenian fortifications, frantically trying to dislodge Demosthenes and his men before the rest of the Athenian fleet showed up, but failed to do so. The morning after their arrival the Athenian ships sailed into the harbour, as the Spartans had not blocked the entrances as was intended. Indeed, when the fleet arrived, the Spartans were still in the process of manning their ships and putting them out to sea. The Athenian ships thus wrought havoc on the Spartan fleet, disabling several vessels and seizing other.

At this sight the Spartans, maddened by a disaster which cut off their men on the island, rushed to the rescue, and going into the sea with their heavy armour, laid hold of the ships and tried to drag them back, each man thinking that success depended on his individual exertions. Great was the melee, and quite in contradiction to the naval tactics usual to the two combatants; the Spartans in their excitement and dismay actually engaged in a sea fight on land, while the victorious Athenians, in their eagerness to push their success as far as possible, were carrying on a land fight from their ships. After great exertions and numerous wounds on both sides they separated, the Spartans saving their empty ships, except those first taken; and both parties returning to their camp, The Athenians set up a trophy, gave back the dead, secured the wrecks, and at once began to cruise round and carefully watch the island, with its intercepted garrison... (Thucydides 4.14.2–5)

Sphacteria with its 400 Peloponnesian hoplites was now surrounded. The remainder of the Spartan forces watched helplessly from the mainland. A delegation arrived from Sparta to assess the situation, and they concluded that there was no way the trapped hoplites could be rescued by force, and so envoys were sent to arrange a truce with the Athenians. A brief armistice was agreed to at Pylos. The envoys were sent to Athens and spoke before the assembly in which they attempted to persuade the Athenians to agree on terms of peace, arguing that the only way the war could end would be via such a treaty.

> Indeed if great enmities are ever to be really settled, we think it will be, not by the system of revenge and military success, and by forcing a opponent to swear a treaty to his disadvantage; but when the more fortunate combatant waives his privileges and, guided by gentler feelings, conquers his rival in generosity and accords peace on more moderate conditions than expected. (Thucydides 4.19.2)

Although these words might seem wishful thinking on the part of the Spartans, a substantial number of Athenians were willing to try to come to terms in order to end the conflict, however others, driven by arrogance, pride and the scent of victory, refused to negotiate terms. It was this side that won out and the Spartan envoys returned home without securing a treaty, a truce or the release of the hoplites on Sphacteria.

When news of failed meetings reached Pylos the Athenians reinforced the blockade, their fleet having been bolstered by an additional 20 ships. Despite this the battle dragged on, with both sides suffering from a lack of resources, and the Athenians becoming increasingly frustrated with the fact that it was taking so long to 'reduce a body of men shut up in a desert island, with only brackish water to drink...' (Thucydides 4.26.4). At this point the Athenians made the decisive decision to land 800 hoplites on Sphacteria, splitting them between either side of the island. They landed at dawn and took the advance post, held by 30 Spartans, entirely by surprise. Shortly afterwards:

> ...the rest of the army landed, that is to say, all the crew of rather more than 70 ships, except the lowest rank of oars, with the arms they carried, 800 archers, and as many peltasts, the Messenian reinforcements, and all the other troops on duty around Pylos, except the garrison in the fort. (Thucydides 4.32.2)

These lightly armed troops harassed the trapped Peloponnesians, forcing them the give ground and retreat. The Athenians wisely maintained their policy of refusing to engage in pitched battle, depriving the Spartans of the only chance they had as 'wherever he went he would have assailants behind him, and these light-armed attackers would prove the most difficult to deal with ... and there being no means of getting them at close quarters, as they could flee if pursued, and the moment their pursuer turned they would be upon him' (Thucydides 4.32.4). The Spartans found themselves cornered, wounded, starving, exhausted, and completely outnumbered. At this point, the surviving hoplites were given the option of surrender, as the Athenians wanted to take the Spartans alive as hostages. This led to a flurry of messages being sent back and forth between the dismayed Spartans watching from the mainland, and those trapped on the island, who received the following instructions 'The Spartans bid you to decide for yourselves so long as you do nothing dishonourable' (Thucydides 4.38.3). This advice was not exactly helpful or uplifting, and so the last 292 Peloponnesian hoplites on Sphacteria surrendered to the Athenians. 120 of them were Spartans. This was a triumphant moment for Athens: not only had they established a fortified base at Pylos from which they could attack the Peloponnese, they had also won a significant strategic victory over Sparta. Spartans were not supposed to surrender, and the fact that they did was a massive moral and psychological blow.

The events at Pylos and Sphacteria certainly gave Athens the upper hand. In 424 the Spartans did not invade Attica, fearing the Spartan hostages would be executed, and indeed this was the Athenian plan as 'the Athenians determined to keep them in prison until the peace, and if the Peloponnesians invaded their country in the interval, to bring them out and put them to death' (Thucydides 4.41.1). Instead, the Athenians went of the offensive: taking the island of Cythera off the southern coast of Laconia. With both Cythera and Pylos as a base, the Athenians and their allies (particularly the Messenians from Naupactus) began to raid Laconian territory doing exactly the same thing the Spartans had done to Attica. In other words, the tables had turned. The Spartans were rattled, but attempted to counter the Athenian raids by sending:

> ...garrisons here and there through the country, consisting of as many hoplites as the points menaced seemed to require, and generally stood very much upon the defensive. After the severe and unexpected blow that had befallen them on the island, the occupation of Pylos and Cythera, and the apparition on every side of a war whose rapidity defied precaution, they lived in constant feat of internal revolution and now took the unusual step of raising 400 horse and a force of archers, and became more timid than ever in military matters, finding themselves involved in a maritime struggle, which their organisation had never contemplated... (Thucydides 4.55.1–2)

The Athenian fleet progressed along the east coast of the Peloponnese, taking the city of Thyrea and its Spartan garrison. The inhabitants of the town were refugees from Aegina (who had defected from Athens earlier in the war); they found themselves at the mercy of the Athenians who killed many on the spot, while the rest were sent back to Athens for public execution. This was a clear echo of the treatment given to the Plataeans by the Spartans and Thebans only a few years earlier.

Sparta rallies: Megara, Delium and Amphipolis

The Athenians moved on to Megara. There was no love lost between the Athenians and the Megarians. The Athenians seized the nearby port of Nisaea and its Peloponnesian garrison, but the city of Megara itself avoided capture. This was due to the actions of the Spartan general, Brasidas, who happened to be nearby gathering troops. He quickly put together a sizeable force of hoplites as well as some Boeotian cavalry with which he halted the Athenian advance on the city. Brasidas and his army arrived at Megara, where the Athenian light troops, who were spread out over the plain, were caught by surprise when the Boeotian cavalry attacked them. Only the intervention of the Athenian cavalry saved them, and what should have been a short skirmish in favour of the Boeotians turned into a lengthy cavalry battle that ended in a stalemate with both sides claiming victory. After this Brasidas moved closer to the city and drew up his lines for battle, but did not advance. The Athenians likewise formed up, but would not initiate battle, as their generals were feeling cautious about their prospects of success and did not dare risk defeat. This stalemate was enough to turn the Athenians away and they withdrew from Megara, turning their attention north to Boeotia and the Thebans. They planned to unleash several simultaneous attacks on the region and wanted to fortify the coastal town of Delium. It was a failed attempt from the outset as things went awry from the beginning when their plans were leaked, allowing relief forces to come to the aid of the targeted cities, although they did manage to fortify Delium. This spurred the Boeotians into action and a coalition force consisting of '7,000 hoplites, more than 10,000 light troops, 1,000 horse, and 500 peltasts' (Thucydides 4.93.3) formed up against the Athenians whose 'hoplites throughout the whole army formed eight deep, being in numbers equal to the enemy, with the cavalry upon the two wings' (Thucydides 4.94.1). The Boeotians launched the attack and the Athenians advanced at a run against them. Thucydides provides us with a vivid description of the ensuing battle:

> The extreme wing of neither army came into action, one like the other being stopped by the water courses in the way; the rest engaged with the utmost obstinacy, shield against shield. The Boeotian left, as far as the center, was worsted by the Athenians. The Thespians in that part of the field suffered most severely. The troops alongside them having given way, they were surrounded in a narrow space and cut down fighting hand to hand; some of the Athenians also fell into confusion in surrounding the enemy and mistook and so killed each other. In this part of the field the Boeotians were beaten, and retreated upon the troops still fighting; but the right, where the Thebans were, got the better of the Athenians and shoved them further and further back, though gradually at first. It so happened also that Pagondas [the Boeotian commander], seeing the distress of this left, had sent two squadrons of horse, where they could not be seen, round the hill, and their sudden appearance struck a panic into the victorious wing of the Athenians, who thought that it was another army coming against them. At length in both parts of the field, disturbed by this panic, and with their line broken by the advancing Thebans, the whole Athenian army took flight. Some made for Delium and the sea, some for Oropus, others for Mount Parnes, or wherever they had hopes of safety, pursued and cut down by the Boeotians, and in particular by the cavalry… (Thucydides 4.96.2–8)

Nearly 1,000 Athenians died in this battle, including their general Hippocrates. The Boeotians then advanced on Delium attacked the fortifications, which they succeeded in taking by creating what was in effect a form of flamethrower that was used to set fire to the walls. One of the Athenians who fought at Delium was none other than the famous philosopher, Socrates.

The Spartans, although stinging from Sphacteria, did not spend 424 entirely inactive, even though they did not make their accustomed raid into Attica. Instead they looked farther north to the Chalcidice Peninsula, which formed an important yet vulnerable part of the Athenian empire, and had already proved to be a headache for the Athenians, particularly in the early stages of the war when Potidaea and several other cities in the region rose up in rebellion against Athenian hegemony. The Spartan general Brasidas marched with an allied force and financial backing from both Macedonia and the League of the Chalcidice, both of which were keen to remove Athenian control from the area. Brasidas persuaded the cities of Acanthus and Stageira to revolt, then he marched on Amphipolis, a city founded by the Athenians in 437/6. Located on the Strymon River, Amphipolis provided a strategic access point for the regions rich natural resources, namely gold and timber, while also serving as a barrier of sorts against incursions from Thrace. The sudden appearance of Brasidas and his troops caught the citizens of Amphipolis entirely off guard. Brasidas seems to have been hopeful that a group of traitors within the city would open the gate, allowing him to take the city peacefully. Instead, the defenders sent a message to the Athenian commander Thucydides (the author of the *Peloponnesian War*) who was stationed nearby at Thasos. Upon learning that aid was en route to the city, Brasidas took the initiative and offered the inhabitants reasonable terms, which they accepted. Thus, despite his best attempt, Thucydides was unable to reach Amphipolis in time to prevent its surrender, and his failure resulted in exile.

The Athenians were troubled by Brasidas' presence and action in the Chalcidice. The loss of Amphipolis was a huge blow. They were quite concerned that '…more allies would revolt, particularly because Brasidas had displayed such moderation in all his conduct, and declared everywhere that he had been sent out to free Hellas' (Thucydides 4.108.2). In 423 the two sides came to a very hesitant truce, agreeing to a year long peace treaty. Both sides agreed to stop incursions into enemy territory and placed a ban on accepting deserters. The truce was really only a window dressing: conflict continued in fits and starts with Athens looking towards Sicily, and the Boeotians continuing to cause trouble for the Athenians. At the same time there was a push in Athens to send a force to recapture Amphipolis. The

Athenian general Cleon set sail with a force of 1,200 hoplites, 300 cavalry, a large contingent of allies, and 30 ships, heading first for Thrace and from there to Amphipolis, where Brasidas had established a base with a large force that included Thracian mercenaries, Chaldician allies, and well as Greek hoplites and cavalry. Cleon advanced towards the city ostensibly to scout it out, apparently not actually intending the fight. Brasidas seized the advantage and planned an attack. When Cleon realized what was about to happen, he attempted to retreat as he wanted to avoid a battle until further reinforcements arrived. As soon as the Athenians began their retreat, Brasidas launched a two-pronged attack. He '…fell upon and routed the center of the Athenians, panic-stricken by their own disorder and astounded at his audacity' (Thucydides 5.10.6), at the same time, a second detachment hit the Athenians, causing them to be assailed on both sides. The Athenian force broke into confused flight; a significant number of hoplites were cut down, as was Cleon. The battle was a resounding victory for the Spartan side; however, Brasidas was also killed in the fighting thereby depriving the Spartans and their allies of a very competent general.

The death of Brasidas and the Athenian's failure to re-take Amphipolis caused both sides to pause and take stock of the situation. The war had been ongoing for 10 years and was clearly at a stalemate. The Spartans were suffering from a severe shortage of manpower, still had hostages in Athenian hands, their fleet had been destroyed – they had begun rebuilding it after the capture of Amphipolis but were clearly not a naval threat, and were dealing with a helot uprising at home. The Athenians were suffering financially as several states had broken from the empire, depriving Athens of their tribute. Power in Athens was shifting from the war-mongering side to a far more cautious and pragmatic approach, led by Nicias, who played a major role in the ensuing peace treaty, the 'Peace of Nicias,' in 422/1. The premise to the treaty was similar to the Thirty Years Peace, but would be implemented for 50 years. There was a general exchange of prisoners. Both sides were to give up territory gained in the course of the war, but the Athenians refused to give up the port of Nesaea, and the Thebans Plataea. Amphipolis was returned to the Athenians, but the other cities of the Chalcidice retained their freedom. The Spartans received Pylos and Cythera. Athens and Sparta also created a separate treaty, which stated that Athens would aid Sparta in the event of a helot uprising. Thus, after 10 years of fighting things came to a momentary halt. For all intents and purposes things had come to a stalemate. The Spartans and Peloponnesian League had not been entirely successful in their mission to free the oppressed cities of the Athenian empire and curb the imperialistic tendencies of Athens; at the same time, Athens had taken some definite losses with regards to subject states and their tribute.

War resumes: Corinthians, Argives and Mantinea

Needless to say, the Peace of Nicias did not last 50 years This was due in part to the perpetually simmering suspicion between Athens and Sparta, but an added and not insignificant issue was the refusal of certain allied states – notably the Boeotians and Corinthians – to follow the conditions of the Peace; rather, they kept antagonising the Athenians by ignoring the treaty terms. The Corinthians, who up until now had been solid allies of Sparta, were so displeased by the peace that they went to Argos, Sparta's traditional foe within the Peloponnese, and:

> ...opened negotiations with some of the men in office there, pointing out that Sparta could have no good end in view, but only the subjugation of the Peloponnese, or she would never have entered into a treaty and alliance with the once detested Athenians, and that the duty of consulting for the safety to the Peloponnese had now fallen upon Argos... (Thucydides.5.27.2)

They encouraged the Argives to invite other states to join with them to create a defensive alliance with the purpose of preventing Sparta from expanding their control and powers. The Argives agreed to this plan and one of the first cities to defect from the Peloponnesian League to join Argos was Mantinea, causing the rest of the Peloponnese to sit up and take notice. The Spartans tried to force Corinth back into line as they were the instigators of all this, but the Corinthians declared that Sparta's treaty with Athens was an abomination and went against the oaths they had sworn. As the new alliance grew the Argives became spooked, fearing that if things went wrong they would end up isolated and surrounded by Sparta and her allies, so in the summer of 420 they opened negotiations with Sparta to see if it was possibly to create a treaty of their own.

In Athens the treaty with Sparta was not unanimously accepted, and there was a party who were eager to declare it null and void. This group was led by Alcibiades, an up and coming military figure and the nephew of Pericles. At Alcibiades' insistence the Athenians opened negotiations with the Argives. In Argos this idea was met with favour and they immediately dropped their plans for an alliance with Sparta in favour of one with Athens. They agreed to a hundred year truce between the cities of Athens, Argos, Elis, and Mantinea. Once again, Corinth found themselves in a sticky situation: they had denounced the treaty between Sparta and Athens, and now they found themselves in the same situation once again, in essence 'The Corinthians thus stood aloof from their allies…' (Thucydides 5.48.3).

In 419 the Argives attacked the city of Epidaurus, which served as a buffer against the Corinthians and was a strategic spot from which the Athenians could enter the Peloponnese. In response to the Argive attack, the Spartans sent aid to the Epidaurians, a move that the Athenians claim broke the truce. The Spartans gathered together an allied force, led by king Agis, with the intent of launching an attack on Argos, which the Argives prevented by pushing further into the Peloponnese to cut the allies off. Agis managed to surround the Argive army, but instead of pushing them to battle he made terms (an action for which he took a lot of flak back at home). The Argives negated these terms in 418 when they once again set out in an attempt to persuade other Peloponnesian states to switch sides and join the Athenian cause. Having stirred up some trouble, the Argives moved into Mantinea, from where the intended to focus their attention on the city of Tegea, one of Sparta's primary allies. The Spartans could not ignore this direct threat and mobilized a force to deal with it 'Upon this news a force marched out from Sparta of Spartans and Helots and all their people immediately and upon a scale never before witnessed' (Thucydides 5.64.2). Agis once again led the attack: he was bound and determined to force the enemy out into pitched battle by ravaging Mantinean territory. It worked, to a certain extent. The Argives, Mantineans and their allies sallied out, but not to face Agis directly. Instead they took a defensive position with the intention of forcing Agis to make the first move. The plan almost worked, Agis made a move to march on them, despite the fact that they held the better ground. However, one of the Spartan elders with Agis called him out on his rash and foolhardy mistake. Agis sensibly heeded this advice and retreated to Tegea. Agis took a new approach and determined to shift his opponents from their position by manipulating their water sources, diverting the river Ophis so that it would flood the plains with the arrival of the autumn rains. Agis' thought was that the threat of this destruction would force the Mantineans down from the high ground onto the plain, putting them on level ground with his army. While Agis was making these plans, the Argives decided to risk battle with the Spartans and moved down to the plain, along with their allies. Agis and the Spartans were unaware of this significant move, and were caught surprised when they found the enemy drawn up for battle, indeed 'A shock like that of the present moment the Spartans do not ever remember to have experienced. There was scant time for preparation, as they instantly and hastily fell into their ranks' (Thucydides 5.66.2).

Agis arranged his forces as per Spartan tradition. The Spartan and Laconian hoplites held the center, the Arcadian allied hoplites on both wings, with the freed helot hoplites also on the left wing. At the edges of each wing were small numbers of Spartan cavalry along with light-armed infantry. On the opposite side, the Mantineans held the right wing with some Arcadian hoplites. Next to them stood 1,000 elite Argive hoplites, while the majority of the Arcadian hoplites took the center and right wing; the right was further bolstered by 1,000 Athenian hoplites and cavalry. Having drawn up their lines they joined battle:

> ...the Argives and their allies advancing with haste and fury, the Spartans slowly and to the music of many flute players – a standing institution in their army, that has nothing to do with religion, but is meant to make them advance evenly, stepping in time, without breaking their order, as large armies are apt to do in the moment of engagement. (Thucydides 5.70.1)

As the two sides moved towards each other the lines began to drift right – this was typical in hoplite warfare as the men shifted their unprotected right side into/behind the shield of the man next to him. A sizeable gap appeared in the Spartan line, which the Mantineans and the Arcadians on the right, along with the elite Argives, pushed through towards the baggage lines; however, their center and left were struggling, with the Athenians on the left encircled by the enemy; only the cavalry on the left prevented a total rout. At this stage in the battle both sides were holding victorious in one part of the field, but struggling elsewhere. Agis made the decisive choice to turn the bulk of his army back against the Argives, Arcadians and Mantineans who had pushed through his lines, encircling them and shifting the tide of battle to his favour. The Argives were able to get away, but the others all suffered heavy losses. The battle of Mantinea was one of the largest engagements of the Peloponnesian War. It vindicated the Spartans and restored their reputation as a military power, but it did little to ease the tensions and conflicts between the two sides.

In the summer of 416, the Athenians sent a naval expedition against Melos, an island that refused to submit to Athenian control, in part because the Melians were a Spartan colony, however they had remained neutral throughout the course of the war by refusing to engage in combat. Their fleet consisted of 38 ships, 1,600 Athenian hoplites, 300 archers, 20 mounted archers and an additional 1,500 allied hoplites. Instead of attacking the island forthwith, the Athenians sent envoys to negotiate with the Melians. From the start the Melians made it clear that they saw the situation in black and white, stating that their only options were war or slavery for '…all we can reasonably expect from this negotiation is war, if we prove to have right on our side and refuse to submit, or in the contrary case, slavery' (Thucydides 5.86.1). The debate between the two sides is known as the Melian Dialogue and reads as a series of sharp ripostes arguing both practical and moralistic defenses in an attempt to outwit each other, while also highlighting the increasing 'us or them' attitude held by the Athenians. The Melians concluded that they had no choice but to reject an Athenian alliance in favour of freedom and resolved to trust in 'the fortune by which the gods have preserved it until now, and in the help of men, that is the Spartans; and so we will try to save ourselves' (Thucydides 5.112.2). The Athenians immediately lay siege to Melos and in the winter of 416/15, partly on account of treachery from within the city, Melos fell to the Athenians. Unlike with Mytilene, there would be no mercy shown this time: the men were executed, the women and children sold into slavery, and the island re-colonized.

Sicily

Back in Athens some interesting things were starting to happen. In the spring of 415 they received an embassy from the city of Egesta in north-western Sicily. The Egestans were having some issues with their neighbours in the city of Selinus, and they had the idea that the Athenians might be willing to sail to Sicily in order to help them out. Now, the Egestans recognized that the Athenians were not going to do this purely out of goodwill; they would expect something in return, especially as they were already embroiled in an increasingly allout war at home. Given the tight financial situation in Athens the most tantalising thing the Egestans could offer was money. To win the Athenians over the Egestans invited an embassy to come visit their city: they wanted to give the impression that Egesta was wealthy enough to support an expedition, and further, that Sicily was chock full of money, thereby peaking Athenian interest in the island by making it seem like it was entirely in the self-interest of the Athenians to get involved in Sicilian affairs. Unfortunately for the Athenians, the Egestans had rather misrepresented the amount of funds at their disposal, a factor that would not be discovered until it was too late. When the embassy returned to Athens from Sicily they prevented the evidence as they had seen it and the matter was put to a vote: should Athens send an expedition to the aid of the Egestans, or not. On the one side was the pro-war group, led by Alcibiades. They pushed the idea that Sicily was a rich territory prime for Athenian intervention as it was full of internal strife and weak cities; essentially easy pickings. On the other side were those opposed to these imperialistic tendencies, who argued that Athens was already embroiled in a war at home, and that it would be foolhardy to spread their resources thin by trying to fight on two fronts. This group was led by the ever-cautious Nicias. Ultimately it was the imperialistic argument of conquest that won out, and the Athenians voted to send a fleet under the joint command of Alcibiades and Nicias, as well as a third individual, Lamachus (perhaps hoping they would balance each other out) to Sicily. Athens threw itself wholeheartedly into the expedition, sparing no expense on the fleet. They gave three goals for this expedition: to help Egesta, to re-establish the city of Leontini which had fallen under the control of Syracuse (Leontini had previously applied for help from the Athenians, and they had supported the Egestans in their request for aid from Athens), and finally, they were to act in the best interest of the Athenians. At the end of the day, this final purpose seems to have been the overarching purpose of the Sicilian campaign.

The expedition got off to an inauspicious start. Just before the fleet was due to set sail a rather alarming and blasphemous event occurred: the desecration of the herms (ithyphallic busts of the god Hermes placed at crossroads and other locations in the

Athenian tetradrachm depicting the Attic owl. Coins minted in Athens became the standard currency within the Athenian empire. (Getty Museum Open Content Program)

city). This desecration was a big deal as many Athenians thought it indicated the expedition was ill-omened. The individual accused of being the ringleader in this act was non other than Alcibiades, the pro-imperialist whose arguments secured the vote in favour of this endeavour, and further, who was sailing as one of the commanders.

The Athenian expedition that landed on Sicily in 415 consisted of:

> ...134 triremes in all (beside 2 Rhodian penteconters) of which 100 were Athenian vessels – 60 men-of-war, and 40 troopships – and the remainder from Chios and the other allies; 5,100 hoplites in all, of which 1,500 were Athenian citizens from the rolls at Athens and 700 thetes shipped as marines, and the rest allied troops, some of them Athenian subjects, and besides these 500 Argives and 250 Mantineans serving for hire, 480 archers in all, 80 of whom were Cretans, 700 slingers from Rhodes, 120 light armed exiles from

Megara, and 1 horse transport carrying 30 horses. (Thucydides 6.43.1)

Upon landing on the island, the Athenians quickly realized there were actually no funds to support their endeavours. They were further disheartened when it became clear that winning the cooperation of the Sicilian cities was going to be more difficult than anticipated. The three generals had very different ideas on how to proceed: Nicias wanted to deal with Selinus and head home, Alcibiades proposed sending out heralds to all of the Sicilian cities (except Selinus and Syracuse) offering up an alliance, while Lamachus thought they should make straight for Syracuse and attack before they were able to properly prepare themselves for battle. Alcibiades won out and he set off to try and drum up support for an alliance, meeting with only moderate success and much resistance. In the meantime, Alcibiades was still under great suspicion back in Athens and the decision was made to bring him to trial. A ship was sent to fetch him back from Athens, 'with instructions to order him to return and answer the charges against him, but not to arrest him, because they wished to avoid causing any agitation in the army or among the enemy in Sicily...' (Thucydides 6.61.4–5). Alcibiades willingly agreed to their request, but as soon as they set sail, broke away in his own ship and fled to Sparta.

The most significant proponent of the Sicilian expedition, the driving force behind the whole thing, was now gone. Matters were left in the hands of Nicias and Lamachus, with the former having been the most vocal opponent to the plan from the very beginning. In the winter of 415/14 they tested the waters by making a rapid assault on the major city of Syracuse, as it had become clear they would have to make a show of power if they were to have any hope of gaining favour on the island. The gamble paid off and they defeated a Syracusan force outside the city, however the Athenians were going to need additional resources, especially cavalry, if they were to have any hope of carrying off a successful campaign. Following this attack,

Nicias and Lamachus withdrew their forces to a pro-Athenian town for the winter to make a plan of action. The Syracusans sent messages to the Peloponnese requesting immediate help. The Corinthians immediately agreed to support their cause and sent envoys of their own with the Syracusans to help plead their case in Sparta. Their biggest supporter in Sparta turned out to be the fugitive Alcibiades, who spoke before the assembly and explained the real purpose for the expedition to Sicily.

> We sailed to Sicily first to conquer, if possible, the Sicilians, and after them the Italians also, and finally to assail the empire and the city of Carthage. In the event of all or most of these schemes succeeding, we were then to attack the Peloponnese, bringing with us the entire force of the Hellenes lately acquired in those parts, and taking a number of barbarians into our pay, such as the Iberians and others in those countries, recognised as the most warlike

Alcibiades was an Athenian politician and general raised in the house of Pericles. A close friend of Socrates and the quintessential Athenian playboy, he was one of the most colourful figures in Greek history. Alcibiades was a vocal supporter of the expedition to Sicily. Following his escape from Athenian custody he made his way to Sparta where he acted as an advisor. When certain actions caused him to lose favour there, he fled to Persia where he attempted to gain support for the Athenian cause, but was unsuccessful. He was then given command of Athenian operations in the Hellespont and won several notable victories. He returned to Athens a hero in 407 and given a great deal of power. His part in the Athenian defeat at Notium led him to retire to Thrace. He was murdered after the end of the war.

known, and building numerous triremes in addition to those which we had already (timber being plentiful in Italy); and with this fleet blockading the Peloponnese from the sea and assailing it with our armies by land, taking some of the cities by storm, and besieging others, we hoped without difficulty to defeat them completely and after this to rule the whole of the Hellenic world. (Thucydides 6.90.2–3)

The sobering speech given by Alcibiades shook the Spartans into action and the voted to send Gylippus, a talented general, to Sicily to take charge of the Syracusans.

The start of 414 brought some good news in the form of 300 talents of silver and 250 cavalrymen from Athens. They had also been able to gather together some allies on the island who were able to provide additional cavalry. In their first season on Sicily the lack of cavalry had proved a thorn in the Athenian side, as they were unable to counter the bands of horsemen sent out by the Syracusans to harass them. The generals made the decision to focus their attention on Syracuse. Syracuse was both a significant Sicilian city, but also the primary ally of Selinus. By cutting off Syracuse the Athenians could prevent them from aiding Selinus, thereby causing Selinus to back off and leave Egesta alone. After all, it was on the pretence of helping Egesta that the Athenians sailed to Sicily in the first place. The Athenians acted rapidly and succeeded in taking Epipolae, the plateau above Syracuse, which they immediately began to fortify. The Athenians then set about besieging the city by building a wall of circumvallation.

As Athenian construction continued at an astonishing rate, the Syracusans stepped up their efforts to stop them, building a counter wall to intercept the one being built by their enemy. When the Syracusans were satisfied with their wall, they withdrew and left a contingent to defend it. Fearing the wall would split their forces, the Athenians made plans to deal with it. They sent a unit of 300 hand picked men and some light infantry to lead an advance attack the counter wall, while the rest of the army marched behind. The defenders were taken entirely by surprise and fled. The wall was demolished. The Athenians had also managed to destroy the underground pipes that carried water into the city. They then returned to fortifying Epipolae. Not daunted by these actions, the Syracusans immediately began to construct a second counter wall, which the Athenians also attacked: the Syracusans were once against defeated, but Lamachus was killed in the fighting. Nicias was now in sole command of the expedition. Following these victories an increasing number of cities were starting to ally themselves with the Athenians, providing both manpower and resources.

Gylippus landed on Sicily in the summer of 414 and immediately set out for Syracuse. He arrived in the knick of time, as the Syracusans were rapidly losing hope and the Athenians close to closing the walls circumvallating the city. Gylippus' arrival gave Syracuse the morale boost it needed to keep fighting, while also throwing the Athenians into confusion, as they had not expected this. Gylippus ordered the construction of a single wall from the city up to Epipolae, which would prevent the Athenians from completing their own fortifications. The Athenians defeated Gylippus in their first battle against each other, largely because the ground chosen had been entirely unsuitable for the Syracusan cavalry. Admitting he was at fault, he ordered a second attack, this time using the cavalry to their full advantage, and soundly defeated the Athenians. Following this victory the Syracusans '…extended their wall up to the Athenian works and passed them, thus putting it out of their power any longer to stop them, and depriving them, even if victorious in the field, of all chance of investing the city for the future' (Thucydides 7.6.4). Aid also came in the form of Corinthian and other allied ships, which were to be used to counter the Athenian fleet anchored within Syracuse's Great Harbour. With the arrival of Gylippus the Syracusans began to focus on their naval forces, as they realized they would have to come to terms with the Athenian fleet in the Harbour. In the meantime, a very ill Nicias sent a message to Athens requesting either substantial reinforcements or permission to return home. The Athenians refused to call off the expedition or to recall Nicias, with the result that the Athenians soon found themselves outmanoeuvred by Gylippus and the Syracusans; forced to give ground and withdraw to the marshy ground west of the Harbour taking up a defensive position.

The Syracusans recognized that the Athenians were masters at sea, yet they knew the only way to remove the Athenian threat would be to defeat them at sea. And so, at the behest of Gylippus, they set about modifying their triremes and adopted new tactics, as they felt this would be the way to best the Athenian fleet. The modified triremes were able to ram the Athenian ships from any side, providing a huge advantage in the confines of the Great Harbour. Initial attacks were a bit shaky, but as they became more confident in their abilities, the Syracusan fleet began to gain ground and in the summer of 413 defeated the Athenian fleet, sinking seven Athenian ships and disabling many others, they were 'now confident of having a decided superiority by sea, and by no means despairing of equal success by land' (Thucydides 7.41.4). However, just as things were looking up for the Syracusans, reinforcements in the form of 5,000 hoplites, a large number of light armed troops, and 73 ships arrived from Athens under the command of Demosthenes, the mastermind behind Sphacteria. Demosthenes immediately went on the offensive in the hopes of achieving a decisive victory. He sent the men out to lay waste to Syracusan territory both on land and by sea, receiving little resistance aside from Syracusan cavalry and javelin-men. He made an attempt to take the counter walls with his siege engines, but was repulsed. Realising that it would be impossible to approach the walls unnoticed during the day, he regrouped and made another attempt with a risky night attack. The endeavour started well for the Athenians, but as they advanced at a rapid pace they began to fall into disarray and were routed by a contingent of Boeotian allies who put them to flight. At this point the Athenian side began to fall apart:

Some Athenians were already defeated, while others were coming up yet unconquered for their first attack. A large part of the rest of their forces either had only just got up, or were still ascending, so that they did not know which was to march. Owing to the rout that had taken place all in front was now in confusion, and the noise made it difficult to distinguish anything. The victorious Syracusans and allies were cheering each other on with loud cries…while the Athenians were seeking for one another, taking all in front of them for enemies, even though they might be some of their now fleeing friends; and by constantly asking for the watchword, which was their only means of recognition, not only caused great confusion among themselves by asking all at once, but also made it known to the enemy…In the pursuit many perished by throwing themselves down the cliffs…(Thucydides 7.44.3–8)

At this point Demosthenes realized what Nicias had known all along, that this expedition had been a monumentally bad idea. Demosthenes came to the conclusion that their only option was to abandon the siege and return to Athens, a solution that Nicias agreed to. In the meantime, further reinforcements had arrived to help the Syracusans. To make matters worse, on the night of their planned departure a lunar eclipse happened: both Nicias and Demosthenes saw this as a sign that their departure was ill-omened, and diviners advised them to wait 27 days before making any decisive decisions about the situation. The Syracusans took complete advantage of this indecision, destroying 18 Athenian ships and blockading the rest within the Harbour. Their fleet rendered useless, the exhausted and battered Athenians attempted to retreat overland to an allied city in the interior, leaving behind their sick and wounded to the mercy of the Syracusans. Thucydides describes their retreat in what is one of the poignant passages of military writing:

The dead lay unburied, and each man as he recognised a friend among them shudder with grief and horror; while the living them they were leaving behind, wounded or sick, were to the living far more shocking than the dead, and more to be pitied than those who had perished. These fell to entreating and bewailing until their friends knew not what to do, begging them to take them and loudly calling to each individual comrade or relative whom they could see, hanging upon the necks of their tent-fellows in the act of departure, and following as far as they could, and when their bodily strength failed them, calling again and again upon heaven and shrieking aloud as they were left behind. So that the whole army being filled with tears and in a distraught state, found it not easy to go, even from an enemy's land, where they had already suffered evils too great for tears and in the unknown future before them feared to suffer more. Dejection and self-condemnation were also rife amongst them…For this was by far the greatest reverse that ever befell a Hellenic army. They had come to enslave others, and were departing in fear of being enslaved themselves: they had sailed out with prayer and paeans, and now started to go back with omens directly contrary; traveling by land instead of by sea, and trusting not in their fleet but in their hoplites. (Thucydides 7.75.3–7)

The retreat was slow and painstaking as the Syracusan cavalry and light infantry continually harassed them from every side. Conditions continued to deteriorate and the two divisions (one under Nicias, the other under Demosthenes) became separated from each other. Sensing the increasing weakness and desperation of their enemy, the Syracusans remained relentless in their attacks, but refused to risk a pitched battle. Demosthenes was the first to surrender; Nicias attempted to negotiate an agreement by offering to pay for the freedom of his men, but this was rejected. He had no choice but to push on towards the Assinarus River where:

…impelled by the attacks made upon them from every side by numerous cavalry and the swarm of other arms, supposing that they should breathe more freely if once across the river, and driven on also by their exhaustion and craving for water. Once there they rushed in, and all order was at an end, each man wanting to cross first, and the attacks of the enemy making it difficult to cross at

Grave stele for Philoxenos. The deceased is depicted in full hoplite panoply bidding farewell to his wife. The Peloponnesian War led to the death of thousands of men like Philoxenos. (Getty Museum Open Content Program)

all; forced to huddle together, they fell against and trampled one another, some dying immediately upon the javelins, others getting entangled together and stumbling over the articles of baggage without being able to rise again. Meanwhile the opposite bank, which was steep, was lined by the Syracusans who showered missiles down upon the Athenians, most of them drinking greedily and heaped together in disorder in the hollow bed of the river. The Peloponnesians also came down and butchered them, especially those in the water, which was thus immediately spoiled, but which they went on drinking just the same, mud and all, bloody as it was, most even fighting to have it. (Thucydides 7.84.2–5)

With his army broken and facing a complete slaughter, Nicias had no choice but to surrender, which he did but to Gylippus, not the Syracusans. They received promises that their men would not be starved or executed, and technically they were not; instead they were sent to work in the quarries, where many died as a result of the harsh conditions. Some of those who survived this ordeal were eventually sold as slaves. Nicias and Demosthenes were executed. News of the disaster did not reach Athens right away, and when it finally broke the Athenians refused to believe what they were hearing. Only when additional messengers arrived bearing the same wretched reports were Athenians forced to acknowledge the sheer and utter catastrophe that had befallen their men on Sicily. It was a huge blow to their confidence and morale. Still, they refused to give up and began rebuilding their fleet, determined to go down fighting.

The final years of war

Alcibiades had, in the interim, made himself quite useful to the Spartans. In 413 Agis once again invaded Attica, but instead of ransacking and withdrawing as per standard procedure, he followed the advice of Alcibiades and established a Spartan garrison at Decelea from which he could send out additional raiding parties to ravage the countryside. Agis also focused on trying to cut off the overland supply routes used by the Athenians. In response to these actions the Athenians were forced to man garrisons of their own in an attempt to halt their enemy, thereby spreading their remaining forces across the Attic countryside, weakening their defenses at home. Things were looking increasingly bleak for the Athenians, but they still refused to come to terms with the Spartans and their allies. In response to this Athenian stubbornness, the Spartans began to build up a fleet as they recognized that the only way to force the Athenians to capitulate was by cutting them off from all their resources, especially the maritime ones. As Agis carried on his attacks from Decelea, the Spartans back home entered into negotiations with Persia to form an alliance in the hopes that this would give them a financial and strategic edge over the Athenians. Nevertheless, the war dragged on for another seven years, mainly in the form of naval conflict, with the Peloponnesians becoming ever more proficient and confident on the water. Athenian resistance finally crumbled with the loss of their fleet at the Battle of Aegospotami in 405.

In the spring of 404 the Spartans marched on Athens and anchored their fleet in the Piraeus. Negotiations for surrender began in earnest. Sparta's allies, especially Thebes and Corinth, pressed them to raze the city to the ground and enslave its citizens. The Spartans refused to go this far. Instead they ordered the Athenians to pull down their fortifications, surrender all but 12 of their ships and to bind themselves to Sparta, sharing the same allies and enemies. Their democratic constitution was replaced by a pro-Spartan oligarchy known as the 'Thirty Tyrants'. Some of Sparta's allies were furious with this lenient treatment, particularly the Thebans, who began an anti-Spartan campaign at home while also negotiating with the opponents of the Thirty in Athens. They had shifted their hatred from Athens to Sparta, and now they were willing to work with the very city they had so recently pushed to destroy. Thus, although Sparta won the war, they also managed to alienate themselves from many of the allies who had contributed in no small part to that victory.

One of the major changes in post-Peloponnesian war armies was an increasing use of mercenaries, both at land and sea. This occurred not just in Greece, but overseas as well, with foreign rulers hiring Greek soldiers to fight for them. The most famous mercenary force of the time was led by the Spartan king Agesilaus who had been hired by the Persian prince Cyrus to aid him in an attempt to overthrow his brother Artaxerxes and claim the Persian throne. Cyrus' plan failed and he was killed at the battle of Cunaxa in 401. The events of the expedition and the trials undergone by the Greek mercenaries can be found in a first hand account of the campaign, the *Anabasis* of Xenophon. The significance of Cunaxa lies in the fact that the Spartans were now more willing to look beyond their own borders. The Peloponnesian War had forced them to take a greater role in Greek affairs, forcing them to shed their traditional inward looking customs. Less than 100 years earlier Aristagoras had approached the Spartans seeking aid in throwing off the Persian yoke, but had been soundly turned away when the Spartans realized that Miletus was located across the Aegean in Asia Minor: their perpetual fear of a helot revolt bound them to Laconia. Now, they were not only actively taking part in campaigns outside of their home territory, they were also being hired to fight in foreign territory for foreign powers. This rapid shift in Spartan foreign policy had significant ramifications on almost every aspect of the state.

Sparta's victory in the Peloponnesian War ended the balance of power in the Greek world, such as it was. However, the Spartans could not easily meet the new demands being placed upon them. Strained resources and external influences weakened the socio-economic balance of the state. The cities of Thebes, Corinth, Argos, and Athens formed a coalition against Sparta, leading to a series of battles known as the Corinthian War

(394–387/6). The coalition was backed by Persia, whose king was becoming concerned with the amount of power wielded by Sparta. It is likely he hoped that by playing the Greek states off against each other, they would keep their attention focused on their own territories, rather than looking across the Aegean towards Persia. Although Sparta emerged victorious once again, it became clear that alliances had shifted dramatically, with Thebes and Corinth – both virulent opponents of Athens during the Peloponnesian War – now siding with them against Sparta. Athens recovered remarkably quickly from its post-Peloponnesian War slump and became more involved in Greek affairs, having thrown off the bloody yoke of the Thirty Tyrants in 403, just a year after their surrender. The Corinthian War ended with Sparta making an agreement with the Persian king. This agreement, known as the 'King's Peace', acknowledged Persia's right to rule the Greek cities of Asia Minor in return for a promise that the Persian king would stay out of Spartan affairs in Greece. The Corinthian War also made it evident that Persia had not forgotten about Greece; however their approach had changed. Rather than trying to conquer Greece via military force, the Persians now turned to bribery and diplomacy by using their gold to fund opposing sides in the ongoing battle for control of the Greek Peninsula.

As Sparta struggled to come to terms with its new role in the Greek world, Thebes began to emerge as the new military power. This was due in large part to the two brilliant Theban generals, Epaminondas and Pelopidas, who revamped the Theban army and developed a new and extremely efficient tactic: the Theban wedge. This formation was executed by the Sacred Band, an elite unit of 300 Theban hoplites, at the battle of Leuctra in 371 and led to a crushing defeat of the Spartans. This defeat was followed up by the Theban invasion of the Peloponnese and the resulting liberation of Messenia. This had a huge socio-economic impact on Sparta as liberation of Messenia deprived them of their helots, destroying the foundation of Spartan society.

CHAPTER 3

THE RISE OF MACEDONIA: PHILIP II AND ALEXANDER THE GREAT

The kingdom of Macedonia

THE REGION OF MACEDONIA, LOCATED IN the northern part of Greece, was always a bit of an outsider in antiquity; its borders defined both literally and figuratively by the looming presence of Mt. Olympus. The Macedonians were perpetually viewed as outsiders; the rest of the Greek states never treated them as properly Greek. Although the Macedonians spoke Greek, it was with a particular accent that made them sound a bit different from everyone else. Moreover, Macedonian customs and traditions were viewed as being somewhat antiquated and a throwback to the Homeric age of heroes as found in the *Iliad* and *Odyssey*: for example, a young aristocrat was not considered a true Macedonian man until he had both killed a man in battle and killed a wild boar with only a spear and a net. The Macedonians did such scandalous things as drink unmixed wine, and polygamy was acceptable amongst the nobility. In short, the region was seen as a cultural backwater. In other ways, though, it really was not so different. Particularly when it came to a sense of cohesiveness or unity. As was characteristic of the Greek world, infighting and socio-political rivalries between aristocratic families was commonplace. Even the region itself was divided, into Upper and Lower Macedonia, and although the Argeads ostensibly ruled the kingdom, the Macedonian king most certainly did not wield absolute autocratic power.

Although Macedonia and its rulers were well aware of socio-political and military developments in the rest of Greece, they often had their hands full at home. The kingdom was surrounded by hostile territory which meant it could not always focus its attentions on the Greek world and its happenings; it had to deal with attacks from the Thracians, Illyrians, the Triballi, and other 'barbarian' populations on its borders. However, the Macedonians were not entirely isolated from the affairs of the rest of Greece: they were well aware of the hegemonic and imperialistic tendencies of the Athenians and the Thebans, particularly with regards to the rich natural resources of Macedon. Macedonia sided with the Persians during Xerxes' invasion of Greece. They did this primarily out of self-interest: their main concern was to keep both the Persian invasion and the Greek defense forces out of Macedonian territory in order to protect their own resources. The Macedonians went so far as to advise the Athenians that their best course of action was to submit to the Persians. When the Peloponnesian War took hold of Greece, the Macedonians managed to stay out of the direct conflict: led by their king, Perdiccas II, the Macedonians continually shifted their support between Athens and Sparta based on the current state of affairs. Perdiccas took this course of action for much the same reason as his predecessor during the Persian Wars: above all he was concerned with protecting his own territory.

Philip II

The man who is largely responsible for placing Macedonia at the forefront of Greek affairs was Philip II, the youngest of three sons born to Amyntas and Eurydice. Philip was not meant to be king, but a series of events put him in that position. His eldest

Tetradrachm of Philip II. Philip is largely responsible for changing the course of Macedonian and Greek history. (Yale University Art Gallery Open Content Program)

brother and Amyntas' successor, Alexander II was murdered shortly after taking the throne, he was succeeded by the middle brother Perdiccas III, who died in 360/59 during a battle with the Illyrians. Perdiccas III left behind his son, Amyntas as heir, but as he was much too young to rule, and so Philip was named regent. Philip was an excellent choice, particularly given the immediate and ongoing threat from the Illyrians on their border. Philip was very much a military man: an astute tactician and student of the military arts. He had spent several of his teenage years (368–365) as a political hostage in Thebes. At that time Thebes was the pre-eminent power in Greece, having defeated the Spartans at the Battle of Leuctra in 371. These years were absolutely formative for Philip's later accomplishments and military reforms. He was able to witness firsthand the training and organization of the army, and to pick the brain of the great Theban general Epaminondas who, along with Pelopidas, was responsible for Thebes' military triumphs. When Philip returned

Bronze bit. The horse was central to Macedonian life and warfare. This style of bit came predominantly from northern Greece. (Metropolitan Museum of Art Open Content Program)

to the Macedonian court, he brought this valuable knowledge with him.

Macedonia was horse country, thus, the mainstay of the Macedonian army was its cavalry, particularly the Companion Cavalry who formed the imperial guard that rode into battle with the king, who himself traditionally fought from horseback. Philip was the first ruler to focus his attention on infantry. He established a unit of elite foot soldiers, the *pezhetairoi* (foot companions, although over time the meaning of this term changed and it came to refer in general to Macedonian infantry drawn from the territorial levies). By the time of Philip's son, Alexander III (better known as Alexander the Great), the elite infantry became known as the *hypaspistai* (shield bearers), which were divided into the regular hypaspists and the royal hypaspists. However, the quintessential Macedonian infantryman was the *sarissaphoroi* (sarissa bearers), who carried the sarissa, a 4.5–5.5m long lance made of cornel wood tipped with a foot long metal spear head and foot long butt spike, weighing approximately 6kg. The sarissa and subsequent development of the sarissa phalanx is perhaps Philip's most famous contribution to ancient warfare and it was the foundation of his military reforms. Instead of the more frontal facing position as used by the traditional hoplite, the sarissa phalangite adopted a sideways stance, with the left shoulder facing towards the front of the phalanx, presenting a very narrow target. Wielding the sarissa required two hands on account of its weight and length, which made it impossible to use the cumbersome hoplite shield. Instead, the sarissa phalangite used a small, round shield 0.6m in diameter that was attached to his upper arm by a sling. The placement of the shield and stance of the phalangite made a breastplate essentially unnecessary; indeed, the standard armament for a sarissa phalangite was his sarissa, shield, greaves, and a Phrygian style helmet. Although we rarely hear of the phalangites carrying a secondary weapon such as a sword, they likely had one. The majority of the sarissa phalanx may not have worn a breastplate at all, particularly those stationed in the back ranks of the phalanx. If they did wear one, as those in the front ranks may have, it was likely not the leather or bronze variety but rather the light linen version that was surprisingly effective and less expensive to produce. The sarissa phalangite was relatively lightly armed and inexpensive to equip; so much so that he was outfitted entirely at state expense. In other words, Philip created the first professional state-owned standing army. Curtius Rufus provides us with a colourful description of these career military men when he describes the Macedonian phalanx:

> The Macedonian army, grim and rough looking, it is true, covering behind its shields and spears immovable wedges of tough, densely packed men. They themselves [the Macedonians] call it a phalanx, a formation of infantry that steadfastly holds its ground. They stand man next to man, weapons interlocked with weapons. Focused upon their commander's signal, they have learned to follow the

standards, and to keep their ranks; all obey what is ordered. How to oppose, to make circuits, to run in support of either wing, to change the order of battle, the soldiers are as skilled as their leaders. (Curtius 3.2.13–14).

On the one hand, the sarissa revolutionized infantry combat as it allowed the state to equip a large number of men with a relatively small financial outlay. This meant that 'regular' Macedonian men could enlist thereby increasing the amount of manpower the army could draw upon to fill its ranks. On the other hand, however, the sarissa was a deceptively difficult weapon to use: not only did it weigh approximately seven times more than a standard hoplite spear, its length made it awkward and unwieldy to manage. It was easy for the phalangites to lose control of their weapon, tangling the tips or ends of the sarissa together, especially during the all important lowering and raising of the weapons in formation. Regular training was imperative if the sarissa phalanx was expected to operate with any degree of success, hence another reason why Philip's 'professionalization' of the Macedonian army was so important. The sources indicated that Philip 'held constant manoeuvres of the men under arms and competitive drills' (Diodorus 16.3.1). Philip reportedly would make his infantry march 50km with their complete kit (helmet, greaves, shield and sarissa as well as provisions) to increase their endurance and resilience. The sarissa could be broken down into two parts for transport. On the training field, the phalangites would have practiced advancing and retreating over varying terrain, as well manoeuvres such as opening and closing their ranks.

Upon taking the reins of the Macedonian court in 359, Philip was faced with a monumental task, but 'he was not panic stricken by the magnitude of the expected perils' (Diodorus 16.3.1). His first move was to deal with the Illyrian issue, which he did using a combination of military force and diplomacy. Indeed, he dealt with the issue so well, that he was promoted from regent to king. Having secured his Illyrian border, Philip was

Bronze statuette of a 4th-century infantryman. His armour has not changed from that worn by his classical period counterparts. (Walters Art Museum Open Content Program)

able to look elsewhere – specifically south to his border with Thessaly. Philip's interactions with Thessaly set the stage for his involvement with the rest of the Greek world: it all began with an invitation. Fourth Century Thessaly was a region beset by political strife as aristocratic factions in the various cities challenged each other for control. Two particular cities, Pherae and Larisa dominated the socio-political landscape, with Pherae controlling the coast and Larisa the inland plains that made up the Thessalian League. In an attempt to gain an advantage over Pherae, the Larisans turned to Philip and sought an alliance. Philip was more than willing to accept this proposal as there was always the risk that Thessalian affairs might spill over the border into Macedonian territory; therefore, an alliance with Larisa helped to secure his own southern border. The alliance also gave Philip a foothold in the Greek world, a stepping off point from which he could become ever more involved in Greek affairs. Thessaly offered another incentive that must have piqued Philip's interest: their cavalry. The Thessalians were the pre-eminent cavalry force in Greece, and Philip must have seen an alliance as a potential avenue for incorporating Thessalian cavalry into his own campaigns.

After established the Thessalian alliance, Philip looked in a new direction – towards the Chalcidice and Amphipolis. As we saw in the previous chapter, the city of Amphipolis on the Strymon River had been founded by the Athenians, and was strategically very important because of its proximity to the natural resources of the region. During the Peloponnesian War, the city fell to the Spartans, a huge blow to the Athenian cause. An attempt to regain the city failed, and, although the Peace of Nicias nominally gave control of Amphipolis back to Athens, the citizens of the city refused to acknowledge an Athenian alliance. Thus, Amphipolis was a bit of a sore spot for the Athenians, who desperately wanted to regain the city. To achieve this, they turned to Macedonia.

Demosthenes was one of the most celebrated Athenian orators. He was a staunch opponent of Macedonian involvement in Greek affairs, and is best known for his *Philippics*, a series of speeches attacking Philip II. He is largely responsible for proposing the alliance with Thebes that led to the battle of Chaeronea, at which he fought. The death of Philip did nothing to slow Demosthenes down: he now directed his efforts against Alexander. Even after Alexander's spectacular victories in Persia, Demosthenes remained steadfast in his determination to undermine the Macedonians. He eventually went into exile and later committed suicide to avoid capture. His *Philippics* served as the blueprints for the speeches of Cicero against Antony at the end of the Roman Republic.

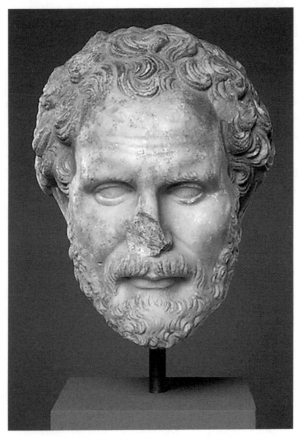

Bust of Demosthenes. This renowned Athenian orator was a virulent opponent of Philip. (Metropolitan Museum of Art Open Content Program)

However, the Macedonians proved unreliable: both Perdiccas III and Philip became embroiled in the Amphipolis issue, and both ultimately acted against the interests of Athens. In 357 Philip secured his control over Amphipolis, and the city became part of his kingdom. This did not go over well with the Athenians, who became staunch opponents of Macedon and Philip.

The first few years of Philip's reign had been busy, and he was not about to slow down. He became increasingly involved in

Greek matters and his next big opportunity presented itself at Delphi. On account of its role as one of the most important sites in Greece, Delphi was not considered the property of any one particular state; instead it was overseen by several different states that together made up the Amphictyonic League. The primary function of this League was to safeguard the sanctuary of Delphi: if the site was violated in any way, the League could come together to declare a sacred war on the perpetrators. It was exactly such a scenario that brought Philip into the picture with the Third Sacred War (355–346), which broke out in response to the Phocians plundering of the Delphic treasuries in order to fund a mercenary force. The Amphictyonic League, led by the Thebans and later joined by the Thessalians, had attempted to deal with the Phocians on their own, but had thus far been unsuccessful; so they turned to Philip for aid. The Macedonians initially struggled against the Phocians, who were led by the very able Onomarchus, however the tides turned in 353 when Philip crushed the Phocians at the Battle of the Crocus Field. From this point onwards, Philip played an increasingly important role in the area and by 346 he was the undisputed master of Northern Greece and leader of the Amphictyonic League. At this point Philip began to turn his attention westward towards Thrace and Byzantium as he started to formulate plans for a Persian conquest. Philip was not allowed to focus entirely on this ambitious project: back in Greece a coalition of forces led by Athens and Thebes rallied together to challenge Philip's authority.

The battle of Chaeronea in 338 was a turning point for both Philip and Alexander. For Philip, it solidified his ironclad grip over the Greek states: Athens, Thebes and their coalition of allies had attempted to resist the might of Macedon, and they failed. Although the sarissa phalanx played a pivotal role in Philip's success at Chaeronea, it was the charge of the Companion Cavalry against the Theban Sacred Band that proved a historical turning point. This was Alexander's debut as a cavalry commander, and the task assigned to him was formidable indeed. Remember,

The lion of Chaeronea. This monument is thought to have been erected by the Thebans to honour their dead. (Rijks Museum Open Content Program)

it was the Sacred Band who dethroned the Spartans at the Battle of Leuctra, and they had held the unofficial title of 'most formidable hoplite force in Greece' ever since then. Moreover, cavalry had not been used in such a manner before. Even during the Peloponnesian War, cavalry forces were deployed primarily as scouts, skirmishers, or to deal with enemy cavalry. Never had they been used to directly attack a solid infantry formation like the hoplite phalanx. Alexander and his horsemen were, of course, successful in this bold move. The members of the Sacred Band were killed to a man, and cavalry had a new function on the battlefield. In this way we can see clearly that the Macedonian army of Philip II was revolutionising ancient warfare.

Philip was in many ways a careful and methodical conqueror. His territorial expansion was gradual, taking place over a period of almost 20 years. We do not know what Philip's precise intentions were with regards to the Persian Empire: did he simply wish to liberate the Greek states of Asia minor from Persian rule, as his propaganda stated, or would he have continued his conquest across Persian territory? These questions must remain unanswered as he was assassinated in 336 before he could begin his campaign in earnest. Regardless of Philip's plans for the east, we can say beyond a doubt that his rule changed the face of Greece. Philip had created a unified Macedonian state under his rule. His powers of diplomacy and military acumen had secured his borders against the kingdom's traditional enemies, whilst also allowing him to expand his influence south and east. Macedonia was no longer a backwater territory at the northern edge of the Greek peninsula with its ruler staying largely out of Greek affairs. The kingdom now possessed the most powerful army in Greece, and a permanent/professional one at that. The Macedonian king now directly influenced the politics and affairs of the very Greek states that had previously belittled his kingdom and its traditions. Alexander succinctly and accurately summed up the magnitude of Philip's influence when he exhorted his recalcitrant troops at Opis in 324:

> Philip…who took you up when you were helpless wanderers, most of you dressed in skins, pasturing a few flocks in the mountains and fighting ineptly to protect them from your neighbours, the Illyrians, Triballi, and Thracians. He gave you cloaks to wear instead of skins, led you down from the mountains to the plains, and made you

able to hold your own in battle against your barbarian neighbours, so your safety depended not on your mountain strongholds but on your own courage. He made you city dwellers, and by means of laws and good customs gave you an orderly way of life. He made you masters of the very barbarians who had plundered you earlier of men and property – you who had been their slaves and subjects – and added the greater part of Thrace to Macedonia. Having captured the most advantageous places along the coast, he opened up the country to trade, made it safe for you to work the mines, and made you masters of the Thessalians, who in times past had frightened you half to death. By humbling the Phocians, he made your route into Greece broad and open instead of narrow and difficult. As for the Athenians and Thebans who were always lying in wait for us, he brought them so low, at a time when I was sharing his toils, that instead of paying our tribute to the Athens and obeying the Thebans, it was their turn to look to us for their security. On his arrival in the Peloponnese Philip again put state affairs in order. Appointed as leader with full powers over the rest of Greece in the expedition against the Persians, he conferred as much renown on the Macedonian people as on himself. (Arrian.7.1–5)

Alexander takes the throne

Alexander's ascension to the throne was not entirely smooth. Although he was keen on pressing the Persian campaign, he first had to deal with issues at home in Greece: several states, particularly Athens and Thebes, railed against the new king, denouncing him as too young to be an effective ruler, and uprisings broke out across his territory A lightening march with 3,000 men crushed a potential revolt in Thessaly, with the result that the Thessalians immediately recanted the opinions of the young king and recognized him as the head of the Thessalian League, giving him the same position and power his father had held. From Thessaly he continued south, where a coalition of Athenians, Spartans, and Thebans had formed in an attempt to challenge Alexander's right to rule. This alliance was efficiently hobbled when Alexander called a meeting of the League of

Bust of Alexander the Great. (Getty Museum Open Content Program)

Corinth and was officially acknowledged as both the leader and general of the Panhellenic mission against Persia. The Spartans refused to accept this and remained staunchly opposed to Macedonian rule by refusing to join the League or support the Persian expedition in any way. They were not alone in this: the Thebans chafed under the Macedonian control imposed on them following Chaeronea, and anti-Macedonian sentiments continued to rumble in Athens, exacerbated by Demosthenes who continued to pontificate against Alexander and Macedonian rule in Greece.

Despite the issues simmering under the surface in Greece, Alexander now looked towards his borders to subdue the Triballians and Illyrians. Although the Macedonian army completed this campaign quickly and efficiently, it nonetheless gave rise to rumours that Alexander had been killed. These false rumours provided the Thebans with an excuse to rise up against their Macedonian overlords: in the spring of 335 they lay siege to the Macedonian garrison in their city and announced they were going to prove themselves the true liberators of Greece by eliminating the Macedonians (with the aid of Persian gold, of course). Alexander's response to this was swift and decisive. As with Thessaly, he made an extraordinarily rapid march south. The Theban rebellion was ruthlessly suppressed and the city razed to the ground. It was a clear statement that any resistance to Alexander's rule in Greece would not be tolerated.

The Granicus

The destruction of Thebes solidified Alexander's position: he could now march east feeling that Macedonian hegemony in Greece was secure. In the spring of 334 Alexander crossed the Hellespont with a force of just under 40,000 men:

> There were found to be, of infantry, 12,000 Macedonians, 7,000 allies, and 5,000 mercenaries, all of whom were under the command of Parmenion. Odrysians, Triballians, and Illyrians accompanied him to number of 7,000; and of archers and the so-called Agrianians 1,000, making up a total of 32,000 foot soldiers. Of cavalry there were 1,800 Macedonians, commanded by Philotas, son of Parmenion; 1,800 Thessalians, commanded by Callas son of Harpalus; 600 from the rest of Greece under the command of

Erigyius; and 900 Thracian and Paeonian scouts with Cassander in command, making a total of 4,500 cavalry. (Diodorus 17.3–4).

Alexander's arrival on Asian soil demanded an immediate response from Persia. Although the king, Darius III, did not consider Alexander to be a truly serious threat to his empire, he nonetheless had to send a message to the invader. The satraps of Asia Minor gathered their forces and met to discuss the matter. Two very different opinions were put forward: the very able mercenary general Memnon (a Greek from Rhodes) pushed for a scorched earth policy with the idea that Alexander would be forced to withdraw if provisions were scarce. Memnon 'advised them to march ahead, destroy the grazing land by trampling it with the cavalry, and burn the standing harvest, not even sparing the cities themselves' (Arrian.1.12.9). The Persians were aghast as this idea and 'it is reported that Arsites declared at the meeting that he would not permit one house to be burned by the men posted with him' (Arrian 1.12.10). Memnon's idea was rejected and they marched to meet Alexander at the Granicus River in north western Asia Minor. The Persian force at the Granicus was composed of territorial levies from the satrapies as well as large numbers of Greek mercenary infantry. These mercenaries essentially viewed the Persians as the lesser of two evils, preferring to fight for the enemy they knew (Persia) rather than the one they did not (Alexander). Although these mercenaries were all career soldiers, they found themselves in a difficult position at the Granicus. The Persians did not entirely trust them to remain loyal when fighting against a Greek army. They were particularly suspicious of Memnon, even though he had a long history of fighting on behalf of the Persians. This distrust meant the mercenary infantry was held in reserve and their considerable abilities not utilized in the battle. Instead, the Persians chose to rely on their cavalry as per tradition.

Upon arriving at the Granicus, Alexander found the Persians prepared for battle. His strategy was to attack straightaway, even though it was already afternoon and the Persians held the

Persian horseman. Cavalry was the backbone of the Persian army. (Metropolitan Museum of Art Open Content Program)

more favourable ground on the far side of the river. Parmenion, one of the generals who had also served under Philip, strongly advised Alexander against this plan, recommending that they wait and attack at dawn for 'at dawn we will be able to cross the stream easily and will make it across before they are in formation...For one can see that the river has many deep sports, and, as you see, the banks themselves are high and steep' (Arrian 1.13.3–4). Alexander rejected this advice stating that he 'would be ashamed, after having easily crossed the Hellespont, if this little stream... keeps us from crossing as we are' (Arrian 1.13.6). Alexander went ahead and formed his lines for battle. He himself led the Companion Cavalry on the right wing, while Parmenion led the left. The line was drawn up as follows: on the right wing were the Companion cavalry, the archers, and the Agrianian javelin men; next to these were the 'sarissa' bearing cavalry and the Paeonian cavalry; rounding out the right were the hypaspists. The sarissa phalanxes held the center of the line. On the left wing were the Thessalian cavalry as well as the allied and Thracian cavalry. Additional infantry were stationed between the cavalry of the left and the phalanx in the center. According to Arrian, the Persian force was made up of close to 20,000 cavalry and nearly as many mercenary infantry. The cavalry were stationed in the front ranks along the riverbank, while the mercenary infantry remained behind them. The cavalry on the Macedonian right led the charge into the Granicus against the strongest contingent of Persian cavalry. The Macedonians forced their way across and up the bank, at which point they engaged the Persians in hand-to-hand combat:

> Though the battle was fought on horseback, it looked more like an infantry engagement: in a confined space horses contended with horses, men with men, the Macedonians trying to drive the Persians from the bank and force them into the plain, the Persians trying to deny the Macedonians a beachhead and thrust them back to the river. And in this struggle Alexander and his men gained the upper hand... (Arrian 1.15.4–5).

The tactics and close combat techniques mastered by Alexander's cavalry, coupled with the skill of the light-armed infantry who fought alongside them as *hamippoi*, proved too much for the Persians who, despite their traditional strength as a cavalry force, fell back, causing their center to collapse and inducing both wings to flight. As the Persian cavalry retreated in panic, the Greek mercenary infantry held their lines and were surrounded by both the cavalry and the Macedonian phalanx.

Cities under siege

News of the Persian defeat at the Granicus spread, and as Alexander moved south many cities began to open their gates to him. Some, however, offered stiff resistance. The first city to deny Alexander entry was, ironically, Miletus – the same city that had provoked the uprising against the Persians in the prelude to the Persian Wars. It seems that this time the Milesians were keen to favour the Persians, and felt they could hold out against Alexander, as the Persians would be able to send aid and resources via their fleet. As Alexander marched along the coast his fleet of 160 ships mirrored him at sea, led by Nicanor, but he was hesitant to engage in naval combat. Instead, Nicanor's fleet proved useful at Miletus when they 'anchored their triremes close together at the narrowest point of the harbour's mouth, their prows facing the enemy, and thereby barred the Persian fleet from the harbour and cut the Milesians off from Persian assistance' (Arrian 1.19.3). While the fleet blockaded the harbour, Alexander lay siege to the city, which fell to him. Meanwhile, the Persian fleet, cut off from the harbour and unable to force Nicanor into an engagement, was forced to put in at Mycale for water. In response to this, Alexander sent Philotas with the cavalry and some infantry to take control of Mycale, effectively trapping them on board and withholding access to any supplies. Unable to come to grips with the Macedonians, the Persian fleet withdrew. Alexander then made the controversial decision to disband his own fleet as:

> …he observed that his own fleet was not fit to do battle with that of the Persians, and he was unwilling to endanger any portion of his forces. He also reflected that as he now controlled Asia with his infantry, he would have no need of a navy: by capturing the coastal cities he would dissolve the Persian fleet, since it would find no crews to man its ships, nor would it have any place to land along the coast of Asia. (Arrian 1.20.1)

Farther down the coast Halicarnassus also resisted Alexander, despite the fact that he had easily taken all of the cities that lay between Miletus and Halicarnassus. In the summer of 334, Alexander reached Halicarnassus and began a siege. The city was well defended both on land and at sea, with operations led by Memnon. The inhabitants fought staunchly against Alexander and his siege engines, refusing to back down. Alexander was certainly hindered by his lack of a fleet, while the Persians were able to bring in reinforcements and supplies by sea. On land his troops were slowly making progress and came close to taking the city by force before a halt was called in the hopes that the inhabitants would surrender. At this point Memnon and his co-commander abandoned Halicarnassus and Alexander, for all intents and purposes, took the city and razed it to the ground. Although the citadels were still occupied by the enemy, Alexander 'decided not to besiege them, realising that it would entail no small delay given the nature of their sites and that there was little to be gained now that he had captured the entire city' (Arrian 1.23.5); he had bigger fish to fry.

Issus

As Alexander continued to march southward it soon became clear to Darius III that he could avoid the battlefield no longer. He set out from Babylon in the fall of 333 with a force numbering between 312,000–600,000 (the numbers vary depending on the source), including 30,000 Greek mercenaries. Darius clearly hoped to overawe Alexander with the size of his army, a very visible reminder of the sheer amount of manpower and resources he had at his disposal across the empire. Indeed, Darius likely had every degree of confidence that the would be able to defeat the Macedonian king in pitched battle, particularly as this one would be fought on a much grander scale than that at the Granicus. Alexander received word that Darius had mobilized his forces and made camp on the plains of Sochi, and so he immediately set out with his own army to meet him. Darius, meanwhile, had carefully chosen a suitable location for battle 'having selected a plain in Assyria that was open on all sides, spacious enough to accommodate his army's vast numbers and suitable for cavalry manoeuvres' (Arrian 2.6.3). However, Darius began to question his decision as he awaited the appearance of his opponent, who had been delayed on account of illness and weather. Instead of holding his ground, he decided to search out Alexander's army and force his hand. Darius marched into Cilicia, narrowly missing Alexander who was en route to Darius' previous location. The two armies finally came face to face at Issus on the banks of the Pinarus River, sandwiched in a narrow stretch of land between the mountains and the sea. Strategically, Issus played itself into Alexander's favour as the confined space would not allow Darius to make full use of his considerably larger numbers. Alexander drew up his lines in much the same was as at Granicus: he held the right wing with the Companion cavalry against the mountains, while the Thessalian and allied cavalry were posted on the left alongside the sea and the infantry held the center. There is a particular pattern to the way in which Alexander fought his pitched battles: the Companion cavalry were the attacking force on the right, while the Thessalian and allied cavalry acted in a defensive position on the left and the stolid sarissa phalanx held firm in the center. To the right of the phalanx, the hypaspists served as a mobile connection between the phalanx and the attacking Companions; in a sense, the whole line worked like a whip crack, with the left remaining mostly stationary, the infantry in the center slowly advancing, and the cavalry on the right leading the charge.

As battle commenced Alexander led the Companions straight towards Darius' position at the Persian center. The Macedonian right shattered the Persian left, but the speed of the charge had opened a gap in his own line as the infantry at the center struggled to maintain their cohesiveness while they advanced slowly over the uneven terrain against the Greek mercenaries posted opposite them:

For as soon as the two sides met hand to hand, the Persians posted on their left wing were routed; there Alexander and his men won a spectacular victory. But Darius' Greek mercenaries attacked the Macedonian phalanx where a gap appeared in its right wing; for when Alexander dashed zealously into the river, coming to blows with the Persians posted there and driving them off, the Macedonians at the center did not apply themselves with equal zeal, and when they came to the banks, which were steep at many points, they could not keep their front line in proper order. Spotting the worst breach in the Macedonian phalanx, the Greeks charged right for it. The action there was fierce, as the Greeks tried to drive the Macedonians back to the river and to recover the victory for their own men who were fleeing, while the Macedonians sought not to fall short of Alexander's already conspicuous success, and to preserve the good name of the phalanx, which at the time was spoken of far and wide as invincible (Arrian 2.10.4–6).

After routing the Persian left, Alexander swung around and pushed the Greek mercenaries back from the river before wheeling and charging at the side of their formation, breaking apart their lines and cutting them down. Darius had stationed the majority of his horsemen on the Persian left wing, as the flatter terrain of the seashore was more suitable to cavalry than the rockier terrain next to the mountains. These units initially held their own and pressed the attack on Alexander's Thessalian cavalry, crossing the river and keeping the pressure on them. As soon as they realized that their left wing had collapsed and their center been cut down they wavered and fled, retreating at speed into mountains so that their:

> ...flight was conspicuous and general. The Persians' horses were suffering in the retreat, carrying their heavily armed riders. As for the horsemen themselves, their enormous numbers were creating panic and disorder: retreating along narrow roads, they trampled one another and thus incurred more injuries from their own side than from their pursuers. Meanwhile, the Thessalians attacked them stoutly, so that just as many horsemen as foot soldiers were slaughtered in the retreat (Arrian.2.11.3).

Realising his army had fallen to pieces, Darius fled the battlefield in his chariot, which he then abandoned in favour of a mounted escape. Alexander pursued him furiously until at last he was forced to pull up with nightfall, giving Darius a reprieve and the chance to reach safety. Alexander's resounding victory at Issus was a blow to Darius, but it did not cripple him. He retreated to lick his wounds, but he was far from prepared to cede his kingdom to the Macedonian.

Tyre and Gaza

Issus proved that Alexander was a talented military leader, and moreover, that he was not prepared to withdraw to Europe any time soon. He continued his progress through Darius' kingdom, but instead of turning inland towards the heart of Persia, he remained on the coast, a strategically significant move: Alexander understood that he needed to take control of the coastal towns and their ports so he could effectively hobble the Persian navy. There was no point in his marching inland if the Persian fleet was still able to move at will in the Aegean; as he no longer had his own fleet (and it had been vastly outnumbered to begin with), his only option was to deprive the Persians of their ports. Without access to these ports, the fleet would be unable to sail. The news of Alexander's victory at Issus preceded him: many of the coastal cities were now willing to welcome him with open arms, but not all of them. In the winter of 333/2 Alexander reached the city of Tyre. The Tyrians were not keen on embracing Macedonian rule, nor did they wish to remain under the thumb of the Persians, instead their desire seems to have been neutrality: they wanted to avoid choosing sides or being seen as openly supporting one regime over the other. Thus, although Tyrian envoys had met with Alexander and reportedly agreed to follow Alexander's orders they denied him permission to enter their city and sacrifice to Hercules. Alexander was infuriated by this decision and immediately made plans to lay siege to the city, a formidable task despite his previous successes with siege warfare.

> The city was an island, fortified on all sides with high walls; in addition, Tyre seemed to have naval superiority at that time, as the Persians still controlled the sea and the Tyrians themselves were in possession of a large fleet (Arrian 2.18.2)

The city itself was located 0.8km offshore on a small island, surrounded by walls reaching 45m in height. Alexander had no fleet with which to attack the city, but his solution was ingenious (if not time consuming): he would build a causeway between the mainland and the island.

> There is a spot there where the strait forms a shoal; the section near the mainland has shallows and muddy spots, but near the city itself, where the channel is deepest, the water is nearly three fathoms deep. But there were plenty of stones and an abundance of wood, which Alexander's men laid over the stones. Stakes were easily fixed in the mud, and the mud itself served as a cement to hold the stones in place (Arrian 2.18.3)

This was a risky move, as the Tyrians could see the construction progress and use their ships and artillery to attack the workers. To counter this threat Alexander had siege towers constructed, which were used both to attack the ships harassing the workers and bombard the city walls. Nonetheless, construction was slow. At one point the Tyrians managed to set fire to the siege engines and, in the ensuing chaos, destroy a large portion of the causeway. Despite this setback, Alexander was not swayed from the task at hand. He ordered his engineers to rebuild the causeway and to widen it so that a larger number of siege engines could be accommodated. Once construction was underway he also set about gathering a fleet, as it would be nigh on impossible to capture the city without one. Fortunately, many of the cities that had recently submitted to Alexander had fleets of their own. This meant he was able to put together a fleet of 224 ships, which set out from the port at Sidon to blockade Tyre. The Tyrians were not lacking in naval power of their own and though they were initially prepared to fight Alexander at sea if he should bring a fleet:

> …having unexpectedly caught sight of a vast number of ships – they had not learned before this that Alexander had all the Cyprian and Phoenician vessels – and finding themselves faced with an organized attack – for just before touching at the city, Alexander's fleet had taken up a position, hoping to tempt the Tyrians to fight at sea, and when the Tyrians did not put to sea against them, the fleet had surged forward with a great plashing of oars – the Tyrians decided not to give battle. Having tightly blocked their harbours' entrances with as many triremes as could fit there, they were standing guard to prevent an enemy fleet coming to anchor in any of those harbours (Arrian 2.20.7–8).

In other words, by refusing to sail out and risk battle the Tyrians had allowed Alexander's fleet to hem them in and cut them off from any possible rescue by sea. In the meantime, construction on the causeway continued to progress, additional siege engines were built and brought by sea to Tyre. Blocked in on all sides, the Tyrians had no choice but to attack the naval blockade. Alexander immediately took action to prevent the Tyrian ships from escaping 'he gave orders for most of ships, once each was manned, to take up a position at the mouth of the harbour and thereby prevent the other Tyrian ships from sailing out' (Arrian.2.22.3). The other ships pressed the attack on the Tyrian vessels which then attempted to retreat, but very few managed to escape. According to Arrian, there were relatively few human casualties as the crews abandoned ship and swam to safety, leaving their ships in enemy hands.

This marked the beginning of the end for Tyre. They no longer had a serviceable fleet with which they could hope to lift the naval blockade and the causeway was nearly completed. At this moment Alexander made the decision to bring his siege engines right up to the city walls. He began the bombardment of the fortifications in earnest: first with those on the causeway, then with those stationed on ships. Other ships he filled with infantry. These he sent to the harbours in the hopes they could force an entrance into the city; those equipped with artillery and archers were sent to various spots around the island with the idea that Tyre would be assailed from all sides. His plan worked, the walls were breached, soldiers poured into the city. After a 7-month siege, Tyre belonged to Alexander. The Macedonian king's wrath was unleashed upon the inhabitants of the city. Only the intervention of the Sidonians prevented a wholesale slaughter of the population. As with Thebes, Tyre was meant to be a send a clear message: resistance would be met with slaughter and enslavement.

From Tyre Alexander marched towards Egypt. En route he was forced to halt and deal with the city of Gaza, which had for unknown reasons (particularly so soon after Tyre) chosen to hold out against him. Alexander was warned that the city would be difficult to take by force, as it was surrounded by a stout wall and built atop a high mound. He ordered his siege engines to be assembled and set about planning his siege. As with Tyre, he was not daunted by the magnitude of the task and hand, but relished the challenge:

> …in Alexander's view, the harder the conquest, the more it should be attempted; the exploit would greatly astound his enemies by its unexpectedness, whereas a failure to capture the city, if reported to the Greeks and Darius, would disgrace him. It was decided to heap up a mound around the city so that, from atop this mound, the siege engines could be brought against the walls on a level plane. The mound was mainly raised at the southern wall, where the city appeared more vulnerable. (Arrian.2.26.3)

The effort and resources required to raise the mound were nearly on a par with the construction of the causeway at Tyre. As soon as it seemed the mound had reached the appropriate height, the siege engines were brought forward and the assault on the walls began. Alexander was seriously wounded during the first part of siege: never one to sit by idly, he had taken the hypaspists and rushed to the aid of the Macedonians who were in the thick of the fighting, at which point he was struck through the shoulder by a catapult bolt. Although the Macedonians had managed to breach the walls, they failed to take the city and the Gazans succeeded in burning their siege engines. Frustrated and injured, Alexander nonetheless continued the siege, ordering the mound to be extended and raised to a height of 76m so that the city was surrounded. They also began digging tunnels under the walls, weakening the fortifications and causing the walls to collapse in some sections, while at the same time, the engines fired a barrage of artillery, until the Macedonians controlled a sizeable section of the defenses. Despite this onslaught, the Gazans refused to capitulate and managed to hold out against three attacks that breached their walls. Finally, on the fourth attack:

> …Alexander advanced the Macedonian phalanx from all sides. At one point he threw down the undermined wall, while at another he broke apart a long stretch that had already been pounded by his engines, so that the assault with ladders, where the wall had fallen, was easily managed. (Arrian 2.27.5)

The Macedonians competed against each other to be first up the ladders: they poured into the city, opened the gates and allowed the rest of the army in. Although Gaza had fallen in a considerably shorter length of time (about two months), the obstinacy of its inhabitants frustrated Alexander. As with Tyre, he showed no mercy to Gaza's inhabitants: the women and children were enslaved, and the city re-populated with tribesmen from the surrounding area who were (presumably) loyal to Alexander. From Gaza he continued his march towards Egypt. When he arrived the Egyptians offered no resistance but instead welcomed Alexander with open arms, celebrating him as a liberator and recognising him as the legitimate heir to the pharaohs.

While Alexander was busy with Tyre and Gaza, Darius turned to diplomacy in an attempt to negotiate a settlement. He sent a letter with terms of a sort. In this letter, Darius sought the ransoming of his family, whom Alexander had captured at Issus, and urged Alexander to withdraw back to Macedonia where he could become a friend and ally of the Persians. Needless to say, Darius' requests were solely for himself, nothing suggested he was willing to see Alexander as an equal, nor was he prepared to compromise with him. Alexander completely rejected the 'terms' of the letter. In his response, Alexander made it clear that he was the one with the upper hand, not Darius:

Egyptian cartouche for either Alexander the Great or his son. Alexander was welcomed as a liberator by the Egyptians. (Metropolitan Museum of Art Open Content Program)

> I have reduced a great part of Asia into my power, I have defeated you yourself in battle. Although there is nothing that you have a right to expect from me, inasmuch as dealing with me you have not even observed the laws of war, yet, if you will come to me as a suppliant, I promise that you shall recover without ransom your mother and your wife and your children. I know both how to conquer and how to treat the conquered...For the future, when you write to me, remember that you are writing, not only to a king, but also to your king. (Curtius 4.1.13–14).

Darius wrote back in a slightly more chagrined tone, he once again offered up ransom for his family, one of his daughters in marriage, and to cede some territory to Alexander. Unfortunately for Darius Alexander had already gained this territory through conquest, and so he gave no attention to Darius' request. By this point Alexander had advanced into Egypt and busied himself with affairs there. Darius, however, was not yet prepared to give up on trying to avoid another battle. In the spring of 331 he sent one final letter to Alexander in which he presented exactly the same terms as his previous letter. Once again, Alexander refused to accept these terms. With his negotiations a complete failure, Darius had no choice but to meet Alexander on the battlefield once again.

Gaugamela

In the spring of 331 Alexander left Egypt and made his way back to Asia, heading for the heartland of the Persian Empire: Mesopotamia. It was here that Darius awaited him with his army. This time, Darius wanted to take no chances. He picked his location with great care, striving to gain every possible advantage over his opponent. The chosen location was in the plains of northern Mesopotamia at a place known as Gaugamela. The open expanse of the plains offered Darius the scope to make full use of his large army to envelop Alexander's much smaller one, while also enabling him to deploy his primary attacking arm – the cavalry – to their full extent. The Persians went so far as to level the ground on the plain 'making it fit for chariot-driving and for use by the cavalry' (Arrian 3.8.7). As Alexander advanced through Mesopotamia he captured scouts sent out by Darius, and from them learned that their king had indeed amassed his forces for battle. Four days after crossing the Tigris, Alexander's scouts spotted an advance force of Persian horsemen. Taking several units of cavalry, Alexander immediately charged forward against the Persians, who turned and fled as soon as they spotted their adversaries approaching. Alexander pressed a relentless pursuit upon them, and several Persian horses collapsed from exhaustion. From their riders Alexander ascertained that Darius was close by. Alexander advanced towards Darius' position, then, when he was just under 7km away made camp and set out to reconnoitre the battlefield. Parmenion urged Alexander to seize the advantage and make a night attack on the Persians. Alexander rejected this idea outright, disdaining the notion of stealing a victory through trickery. Arrian states:

> Though Alexander took many chances in his battles, he recognised that the night posed dangers. Furthermore, if Darius were again defeated but the attack came secretly and at night, he would not be forced to concede that he and the men he led were inferior; whereas if Alexander's men should meet with an unexpected reverse, they would find themselves in a country friendly to their enemies, who were moreover familiar with the region, while they themselves, lacking such familiarities, were surrounded by enemies… (Arrian 3.10.3–4)

While Alexander and his men slept within the security of their camp that night, Darius' army had no choice but to hold their position arrayed for battle through the night as they feared Alexander may indeed do what Parmenion had recommended and launch a night attack.

The next day Alexander drew up his battle lines, arraying them in much the same way as he had at Issus. The Thessalian and allied cavalry were stationed on the left wing under the command of Parmenion, while Alexander led the Companion cavalry on the right. Next to Alexander were the hypaspists who, together with the Companions, would once again be the striking arm. The center was held by the sarissa phalanx. Unlike at Issus, Alexander took additional precautions to protect his flanks and rear, as he was well aware that Darius would try to encircle him. Extra units of cavalry were placed at an angle on the edges of

Scythian warrior armed with bow, spear, and axe. The Persian army was incredibly multicultural, drawing on levies from across its vast empire. (Walters Art Museum Open Content Program)

each wing, while several units of Greek infantry were stationed as a rear guard behind the Macedonian center. Darius' battle order was the following:

The left wing was held by the Bactrian cavalry, the Dahae and the Arachosians; the Persians were posted next (their cavalry and infantry mixed together) and next to them the Susians, and next to the Susians the Kadousioi. This was the order of the left wing up to the middle of the entire phalanx. On the right, the contingents from Hollow Syria and Mesopotamia had been posted first, followed by the Medes; next came the Parthians and Sacae, then the Tapourians and Hyrcanians, and finally the Albanoi and Sakesenai. These were the contingents on the right up to the middle of the entire phalanx. The center was held by King Darius, the King's kinsmen, the Persian Apple Bearers [an elite royal bodyguard], the Indians, the so-called displaced Carians, and the Median archers...In front of the left wing, facing Alexander's right, stood the Scythian cavalry, nearly a 1000 Bactrians, and 100 scythe-bearing chariots. The elephants were posted in front of the royal squadron, along with 50 chariots. The Armenian and Cappadocian cavalry had been posted in front of the right wing with 50 scythe-bearing chariots. The Greek mercenaries had been stationed on either side of Darius and the Persians, opposite the Macedonian phalanx, on the assumption that these were the only contingents that could effectively counter it. (Arrian.3.11.3–7)

Alexander' general tactics were similar to those used at Issus: the cavalry and hypaspists on the right would serve as the primary offensive force, those stationed on the left would act as the defense, while the phalanxes and other infantry stationed between them would advance methodically, pressuring the enemy center. Battle commenced with action on the Macedonian right. Alexander advanced with his wing, continually shifting to the right away from the level ground the Persians had painstakingly prepared. Darius attempt to halt him by sending cavalry to outflank him. Alexander's cavalry were 'pressed hard on account of the barbarians' superior numbers and because the Scythians and their horses had been better equipped for defense' (Arrian 3.13.4). Nevertheless, they held their ground and pushed back, forcing the enemy out of formation and into disorder. This had the effect of drawing Darius' cavalry away from his center, weakening his line and creating a gap in his lines. In the center, Darius had unleashed his scythed chariots against the Macedonian phalanx. His intent was to wreak havoc upon their ranks as the men tried to avoid the chariots and their blades, but it did not exactly go as he planned. The light-armed javelin men attacked the chariots as they approached: hurling their weapons and grabbing at the reins to pull them off course. Those chariots that did reach the phalanx did not cause panic, instead, the soldiers separated in disciplined ranks, allowing the chariots to pass through without causing any harm, at which point their were seized by the army grooms. As this was going on, Alexander then led the charge against the Persians with the Companions, hypaspists and part of the phalanx arrayed in a wedge formation against the gap, which had opened up in the Persian lines. They attacked at speed and punched through, with Alexander making straight for Darius. In the ensuing fighting:

> Alexander and his horsemen pressed the enemy hard, shoving the Persians and striking their faces with spears, and the Macedonian phalanx, tightly arrayed and bristling with pikes, was already upon them, Darius, who had long been in a state of dread, now saw terrors all around him; he wheeled about – the first to do so – and fled. (Arrian 3.14.3)

As soon as Darius took flight, so to did the cavalry attempting to outflank Alexander on the right. Alexander immediately took up the pursuit determined as he was not to let Darius escape this time.

While Alexander's strategy had worked well on the right wing, it caused some serious issues for the Macedonian center. As the right wing advanced obliquely across the field the infantry followed them, but the bulk of these units were not able to keep up with Alexander's rapid charge, causing a large gap to appear in the Macedonian ranks. This could have been disastrous, but the Indian and Persian cavalry who charged the gap made the bizarre decision to gallop straight through and head for the

Macedonian baggage train, where they were then attacked by the Macedonian rear guard. While Alexander was in hot pursuit of Darius he received an urgent message from Parmenion on the left wing where the Thessalian and allied cavalry were under extreme pressure from the cavalry on the Persian right. Upon receiving this news Alexander was forced to wheel and turn back to help. However, by the time he arrived, Parmenion's cavalry along with the infantry stationed next to them had halted the Persian advance and the enemy cavalry had withdrawn.

The Persian defeat at Gaugamela was the death knell for the Darius and the Achaemenid line of kings. Babylon opened its gates to the conqueror. Darius was betrayed by his kinsman Bessus, who first usurped and then murdered him; his body was found abandoned in a carriage on the side of the road by Alexander. Bessus was later captured by Ptolemy, one of Alexander's generals, and executed. With the Persian throne firmly in his grasp, Alexander marched into Central Asia, where he encountered stiff resistance – particularly in Sogdia. This he solved through a political marriage with Roxane, the daughter of Oxyartes, a prominent Sogdian. This marriage largely ended the guerrilla warfare Alexander had been trying to quell in both Sogdia and Bactria. He could now turn his attention to the final portion of the Empire: the provinces of Parpamisade, Gandhara, and Hindush.

The Hydaspes

Alexander marched over the Hindu Kush and through the Swat Valley, before arriving at the Indus Valley. Here he fought the last major battle of his campaign, this time against Porus, the Rajah of Paurava. The Battle of the Hydaspes proved to be quite a tactical challenge for Alexander. Porus was camped on the far side of the river with his army as well as his elephants. He had placed guards at the major fording points, depriving Alexander of these easier routes. It was monsoon season and the river was swollen from the rains so the only safe option for crossing would be on ships or rafts made of inflated hides. Alexander recognized that it would be foolhardy to try and cross the river where Porus was stationed as his men would be attacked as soon as they came within range of Porus' army. However, it was the elephants that posed the biggest problem for Alexander,

> ...he imagined that his horses would refuse to set foot on the opposite bank, since the elephants would immediately charge and the sight and sound of the beasts would terrify them; even before that point, he realised his horses would not remain on the hide floats ferrying them across but would panic and leap into the water when they caught sight of the elephants on the other side. (Arrian 5.10.2)

With these factors stacked against him, Alexander was prepared to be both patient and clever. Instead of waiting in one camp, he created diversions. Every night he sent the cavalry to different locations up and down the bank, having them sound as if they were going to attempt a crossing. At first Porus reacted to these movements by sending his elephants to the location to prevent the crossing, but he soon realized that it was all a sham. This is exactly what Alexander wanted. Once Porus became complacent about the night time activities of the cavalry, Alexander made his move. He picked a densely wooded promontory as his crossing point, guessing that the vegetation would provide cover for his crossing. Once his preparations had been put in place, Alexander set out to make the crossing, leaving a detachment in the main camp under the command of Craterus: they had been ordered to remain in place until Porus moved. If he did not move, or left any elephants behind in the main camp, Craterus and his men were to stay put. On the chosen night a heavy rain started to fall, providing additional cover for Alexander as it concealed the sounds of their crossing. Alexander and the hypaspists crossed in ships. They were spotted by some of Porus' scouts, who galloped back to report the news as fast as they could. Alexander disembarked, but mistakenly on an island and not the opposite side of the river. Realising his mistake, he made haste for the shore. In the meantime, the cavalry were struggling to ford the swollen river in the midst of the storm, with the horses barely able to keep their heads above the water as they crossed. Eventually Alexander managed to marshal his force together on the opposite shore. He took his cavalry on ahead and ordered the infantry to march at speed behind them. A small skirmish was fought with Porus' son, who had been sent to try and stop the crossing, the Indian troops quickly withdrew and Porus advanced to meet Alexander, having left a few elephants behind at his main camp to prevent Craterus from crossing the river. When the two armies met it became clear that Alexander certainly had the upper hand with regards to horsemen: his cavalry considerably outnumbered that of Porus. Porus, on the other hand, hoped to negate this advantage with his 200 elephants, which he stationed in the center of his army, in front of the infantry. The cavalry he did have (about 4000 of them) were placed on the wings. Alexander arrayed his men in a slightly different arrangement for this battle. The Macedonian phalanx held the center as per usual, but instead of splitting his cavalry between the two wings, he massed the majority of it on the right, with only one unit on the left, but hidden from view. Porus saw that his cavalry on the left would quickly be overwhelmed by the vast number of enemy cavalry posted opposite them, so he ordered the cavalry posted on his right wing to move to the left, thereby leaving his right wing devoid of cavalry. This is exactly what Alexander wanted. As battle commenced the contingent of cavalry hidden in Alexander's left wing rode out and around Porus' lines, attacking his horses from the rear while Alexander and the rest of his cavalry charged them. The Indian cavalry was forced to split their ranks, deploying in two different directions, throwing their formation into disarray. Alexander's attack was relentless, and the Indian cavalry were forced back towards their elephants.

At that point the commanders of the elephants led the beasts against the cavalry, and the Macedonian phalanx advanced to meet the elephants, hurling javelins at the men mounted upon them, and shooting at the beasts themselves from all sides. The action was like none of their previous battles; for the beasts sallied out against the battalions of foot soldiers and ravaged them wherever they turned, despite their keeping in close formation, while the Indian horsemen, seeing their infantry joining the fight, turned back and charged the Macedonian cavalry. (Arrian 5.17.3)

The Macedonian cavalry came together as one unit and pushed back against the Indian horse, forcing them back to the elephants. The elephants, suffering from injuries, finding themselves confined in a narrow space and with many of the

Alexander the Great was a remarkable man. At the time of his death he had built the largest land empire yet known. In just over 10 years his army had marched over 15,000km from the shores to the Hellespont to the Siwa Oasis, across the Hindu Kush to northern India, and through the barren wasteland of Gedrosia. They proved their mettle in skirmishes, sieges and large scale pitched battles. His men perfected the art of fighting with combined arms: infantry and cavalry working in concert with each other in a way that had never been done before. Alexander had his tried and true tactics, like any general, but he was willing to improvise and take risks in order to achieve victory. He regularly incorporated conquered populations within his army, notably large Persian contingents, creating an army that was ever changing like a chameleon. Nonetheless the Macedonian infantry and cavalry remained the foundation of this fighting force, without whom he would not have been able to accomplish his incredible feats.

mahouts killed began to panic, causing just as much harm to their own side as to Alexander's, however Alexander's men had more room to move and could get themselves out of the maddened beasts' way. Finally, when the elephants were exhausted and no longer posed a threat, Alexander surrounded the Indians with his cavalry and gave the order for his infantry to lock shields and advance. The Indians found themselves attacked from every side and were cut down in large numbers. A gap appeared in the Macedonian cavalry through which the remaining Indians fled. Unfortunately for them, Craterus had just crossed the river and they ran straight into his troops. The Hydaspes was a resounding victory for Alexander, and if we are to believe Arrian's numbers close to 20,000 Indian infantry and 2,000 cavalry were killed in the engagement. From there, Alexander continued across the Punjab, pushing his men ever further into the unknown. They finally rebelled upon reaching the Hyphasis River and refused to go any further. Alexander capitulated to their requests and turned back towards Babylon.

The death of Alexander at Babylon in 323 was entirely unexpected. His generals were completely unprepared. The king had declared no heir, Roxane was pregnant but the child would need a regent. She did give birth to a son, Alexander IV, who was later killed by Cassander, as were Roxane and Alexander's mother, Olympias. Essentially, Alexander's untimely death caused chaos amongst the high-ranking individuals who had served him. These men came to be known as the *diadochoi* (Successors). The period of the Successors (323–301) was a continual series of battles, diplomacy, and political manoeuvring as these men split Alexander's vast empire between themselves, leading to the foundation of the Hellenistic Kingdoms. These Kingdoms expanded and collapsed, split into smaller territories throughout the Hellenistic Period. Slowly they began to fall under the control of Rome: sometimes through political machinations, at other times via conquest. The Ptolemaic Kingdom of Egypt held out the longest, falling to Rome with the suicide of Cleopatra VII in 31/30.

SOURCES

PRIMARY SOURCES

Arrian, *Anabasis of Alexander*

Curtius Rufus, *History of Alexander*

Diodorus, *Library of History*

Herodotus, *The Histories*

Homer, *Iliad*

Thucydides, *Peloponnesian War*

Xenophon, *Hellenica*

Xenophon, *Art of Horsemanship*

SECONDARY SOURCES

Cartledge, P. (2003). *The Spartans: The World of the Warrior Heroes of Ancient Greece*. Overlook Press.

Chianotis, A. (2005). *War in the Hellenistic World*. Blackwell.

Hansen, V.D. (1989). *The Western Way of War: Infantry Battle in Classical Greece*. University of California Press.

Heckel, W. (2008). *The Conquests of Alexander the Great*. Cambridge University Press.

Kagan, D. (2003). *The Peloponnesian War*. Viking.

Rich, J. and Shipley, G. (eds.) (1993). *War and Society in the Greek World*. Routledge.

van Wees, H. (2004). *Greek Warfare: Myths and Realities*. Duckworth.

Worthington, I. (2008) *Philip II of Macedonia*. Yale University Press.

ACKNOWLEDGEMENTS

Writing is very much an all consuming and solitary affair, but I am incredibly grateful to the support offered by my family and friends. Many thanks to Tim Howe for sending the opportunity to write this book my way and for his continued support of my career; to my family for their ongoing belief that I am actually a writer of sorts; to my friends and colleagues for accepting my self-imposed hermit-hood over the past couple of months; and to Lucas for putting up with the explosion of books and general academic-esque disarray of the writing process.

INDEX